# IMPACT

The Powerful Marriage of
Facilitation & Gestalt

PAUL COOPER

# Acknowledgement

*To my indomitable mother*

Gladys Elizabeth "Liz" Cooper
1925-2022

# Contents

# Preface

I always have a hard time describing my profession to other people. On an airplane, in a bar, at a party – whenever I'm faced with the polite but pro-forma question, "What do you do for a living?" I tend to freeze a little. I'm worried that whatever I say will confuse rather than illuminate.

So my mind races as I try to frame my answer around what I imagine this person might understand. If it's one of my mother's friends at the retirement community, I might say, "I'm a business consultant," which is true but bland, opaque, and unhelpful. If it's a professional-looking person, I might say "I'm a facilitator," since many people with office jobs seem to know what that means.

If I accidentally say, "I'm a meeting facilitator," people go down a rabbit hole, fixating on the "meeting" part. They ask if I'm the one who organizes conferences by booking hotels, printing name tags, and handing out branded tote bags, so I have to correct them: You're thinking about a meeting planner. That job requires an attention to detail I could never handle.

Sometimes I'll be talking to someone who might be a potential client, so I'll try something like, "I help organizations improve their internal communication and collaboration." In those cases I'm trying to evoke a picture of their own communication and collaboration challenges. I'm hoping to start a conversation that will make this person find me instantly indispensable, so we can quickly sign a new and lucrative contract together.

Finally, if I meet someone who seems to be in my same line of business, I'll use inside-the-industry lingo: "I'm a facilitator, coach, and OD consultant." People who are facilitators, coaches, and/or organizational development consultants seem to know what that means. These are the only times I can really be sure I'm being understood.

I wrote this book to be understood. I want to tell people what I do and how I do it. But it's not just about me finding my voice: I've discovered some things that could help others too. I'm sharing my knowledge in the expectation that doing so might support someone else. Putting my insights out in the world allows me to be of service.

I wrote a previous book too: You haven't heard of it. In truth, I wrote that one for crassly commercial reasons. I knew that as a consultant I'd have more credibility if I could also tout myself as an author. So I wrote a book to say I had written a book...and I framed it around what I imagined might impress people who could hire me. The result was serviceable, but meandering and dull. My head was engaged in that task, but my heart was elsewhere.

I am writing this out of a place of love, in part because I have so loved this phase of my career. Having just turned 62 years old I feel like I'm finally coming into my own. Act I of the career was a little rocky, as it is for a lot of people: Fresh out of college, I worked as paid staff in two wildly unsuccessful presidential campaigns, and as a congressional aide. Then I bounced around a series of forgettable political consulting jobs before realizing that I wasn't quite suited to the career I had chosen.

# IMPACT

Politics is inherently about conflict, winning and not losing, and pushing other people down to get the outcomes you want. Don't get me wrong: It's a profession that deserves respect, because the stakes are high and (despite the dehumanizing caricatures of vain and power-hungry politicos), I found that most people I met who worked in the field did so for virtuous reasons.

But oh, their behavior. Despite sharing the heartfelt desire to make the world a better place, many of my fellow Democrats and political left-wingers weren't very nice to one another – or particularly warm to me. In those ten years I experienced a version of what Freud called the "narcissism of small differences." People who mostly shared very similar ideologies habitually devolved into feuds, rivalries, and all sorts of pissy behavior. It just wasn't a good fit.

At the same time I was having doubts about my profession I was struggling to find my voice as a gay man. In my personal life, I was utterly lost. I didn't have a clear idea of what "being a gay man" even meant.

I had seen very few noble images of gay people in my childhood and early teens. To the contrary, everything in my world told me some version of "gay is bad, awful, and shameful," and I swallowed those messages whole. My high school and college years coincided with the rise of the Religious Right and the emergence of AIDS, which was just about the worst timing imaginable. I was petrified that I'd be shunned and shamed by my friends and family, and vilified by strangers. I was frozen with fear about "the gay plague," which rapidly turned young healthy men into frail wasted corpses.

Gay life from my cloistered vantage point in the 1970s suburbs seemed like a bloody battlefield strewn with casualties. I crouched low in my foxhole of denial to stay safe, but I was also intensely lonely and frightened. With so much at stake, it felt insane to make myself visible and vulnerable, putting all the comforts of my life at risk. So I hunkered down, and tried not to think about being gay for as long as I could.

# IMPACT

I muddled through my early adult years telling lies and half-truths to my friends and colleagues, while concealing, compartmentalizing, and deceiving myself. I was stuck and sad. I knew I had to make myself whole. I knew I would never be happy until I did.

At a low point, I found the courage to volunteer at Whitman-Walker Clinic, a health care provider founded by gay men and lesbians that had become one of the premier AIDS service organizations in the country. Arriving at the clinic's volunteer training, I firmly intended to sign-up for a safe and easy support job that involved no direct interaction with sick people – and therefore no requirement for me to come to terms with my sexuality or AIDS-phobia. I imagined myself stocking canned goods in an isolated pantry or sweeping warehouse floors. I only wanted to stick one tiny tentative toe – and nothing more – into the shallowest waters of the gay world.

There were about forty of us seated on hard plastic chairs in a George Washington University classroom one Saturday afternoon, listening to tutorials about HIV transmission, the relative risk of various sexual practices, and the latest news about treatment options. I felt grateful that I didn't recognize anyone else in the room, and I only made the most cautious small talk with other volunteers. I remember feeling a creeping desire to skip out early and just forget about the whole thing.

All that changed when two volunteer facilitators stepped up to pitch their program of holding weekly support groups for clients who were newly-diagnosed with HIV/AIDS. The volunteers spoke to us for only a few minutes, but I found them absolutely mesmerizing. There was something different about them that I couldn't fully grasp. Was it the way they talked, or the words they used? Was it their apparent ease in engaging with the group?

I didn't know why, but I found them captivating and energizing. And suddenly I didn't want to be some meek and invisible warehouse floor sweeper. I wanted to be just like them! I experienced a profound "a-ha!" moment that showed me something totally new – a way of being in the world that seemed powerful, confident, and whole. My tentativeness melted away.

I signed up on the spot to be a volunteer support group facilitator, and from the first day I knew the fit was just right. What I experienced during the seven years as a volunteer enabled me to come out fully. It gave me the courage to live in a world with AIDS. It built my self-esteem by letting me help others in profound and meaningful ways.

And eventually, it gave me a new career...the second Act in my professional story. That's because my co-facilitation of weekly support group sessions showed me that I had found my calling. As my colleague Madeline told me one night, "Oh, you're really good at this."

In fact, I was better at my volunteer job than I was at my paid job. I had noticed several warning signs that my career might be on the skids, starting with my bad case of the Sunday Scaries. Every weekend, my stomach churned with anxiety as I envisioned my work week ahead. On Monday mornings I dragged myself to the bus stop like an unwilling hostage. On Friday afternoons I felt euphoric, as if I had been released from prison. The whipsaw of emotions was dramatic, exhausting, and telling.

So I quit and essentially swapped my paid job for my volunteer job. Over the next year I figured out how to get paid to facilitate, while limiting my political work to the occasional weekend as a campaign volunteer.

I was already a good consultant with a wide professional network, so I started getting gigs almost immediately – even though I lacked experience as a facilitator outside of the support group context. Whenever I felt lost, I operated on instinct. I supplemented the education offered by the Whitman-Walker volunteer program with training in related fields, such as focus group moderation and executive coaching. Over time, I built a reasonably successful practice, and I got better at my craft.

Act 3 of my career began in 2014, when I enrolled in iGold, the International Gestalt Organization Leadership Development course, an 18-month program that featured in-person weeklong trainings in five international cities. In three of those sessions, we used our newfound skills to support local organizations in places like Budapest and Cape Town, helping real-life clients through their own real-life challenges.

Like my first day at the Whitman-Walker volunteer training, the iGold program left me both thrilled and confused. The concepts we studied were powerful and intriguing, and every day seemed to produce multiple "aha" moments. But when I reflected on my experiences, I couldn't figure out how to reconcile all those cool new ideas with how I had been working for the previous fifteen years. The classroom seemed incompatible with the real world.

I struggled to fit the pieces together. Gestalt seemed amazing, but was it useful? I experimented and debated with my iGold classmates, many of whom wrestled with the same dilemmas. How could we harness the concepts we were learning in any practical way to help ourselves or our clients?

I found my answer slowly over time: Gestalt is both cool AND useful. When married with the principles of facilitation, Gestalt dramatically elevates me and my practice, allowing me to be far more impactful than I ever was before.

Integrating Gestalt into my world view hasn't just changed my approach to work; the lessons I've drawn have impacted my personal life as well. Now, when conflict emerges with friends or family, I have new and effective techniques to navigate the situation. I call on my Gestalt training to build intimacy with colleagues, and even to manage an awkward moment at a dinner party.

The concepts and approaches of Gestalt and facilitation bolster me in every facet of my life. They help me manage myself, my relationships, and my understanding of the world. They give me valuable insights into what's happening when things get confusing, and newfound confidence about how to proceed. Gestalt helped me connect with others, see the world more clearly, and promote my values more fully than my previous work in politics or government ever did.

The effects of that transformation are visible to others too. My clients see me as more poised and courageous, with the skills to help them get unstuck from unproductive patterns. My friends see me as more centered and less reactive, with a stronger sense of myself and my boundaries.

For me, facilitation and Gestalt are like peanut butter and jelly: Great by themselves, transcendent together, and perfect for any occasion.

And that's what I really want to share: The combination of facilitation and Gestalt changed me. Regardless of where you are or what you do, these ideas can help you too.

You don't have to work as a facilitator to benefit from this. You don't even have to start with much understanding of what a facilitator does or what "Gestalt" means. Regardless of your career or your level of education, there are ideas here that you can use. In fact, I'll bet you'll experience more than a few "aha" moments yourself, when a small insight can make an indelible change in your perceptions.

And that, it turns out, is enough. Most people don't need mountains of new insights to power personal or professional growth. Often, we don't even need boulders or rocks. An insight no larger than a grain of sand can have a profound impact on how we think and behave.

To the uninitiated, facilitation is pretty easy to explain; Gestalt, on the other hand, is cunningly difficult to describe. Taken separately, Gestalt's individual pieces seem banal, obvious, or downright silly. But they are like the makings of gunpowder; inert and unremarkable by themselves, but when they are combined with care and intention the result can be explosive.

Our iGold faculty warned about this paradox at the end of our first week of the course in Amsterdam. Our teacher Jonno Hanafin cautioned us not to explain Gestalt to our spouses when we returned home, because he knew that our explanations would produce blank stares at best.

But of course I didn't listen. When my husband and two friends met me the next day for drinks at an outdoor café, they asked about the course I was taking, so I gamely tried to explain what made this program worth five weeks of my time and thousands of dollars. They took in my words and sat silently. After a few moments, my husband replied incredulously: "That's it??"

Every book I've ever tried to read on Gestalt has failed for similar reasons. Regardless of how much of a Gestalt booster I've become, the great tomes written by the field's wisest scholars have left me more confused than illuminated, and often thinking, "Is that it?" Worse, most of those books are lead-pipe dull. I can't abide another book filled with sentences masquerading as paragraphs and no pictures. Who has time for a boring read?

I'm aiming to be both NOT boring and NOT confusing. I won't even be complete. I won't try to teach Gestalt or facilitation in their totality. I'm less of a scholar and more of a magpie, collecting bits and pieces that attract my attention and cobbling them together into some presentable whole. Along the way, I've tried to strip out all the history and as much confusing jargon as possible.

Filling in all those details is someone else's work. My job is to explain the concepts that have helped transform my practice and personal life in the hope that some of what I share resonates with you.

You might think of this as an appetizer rather than the full meal. I hope to entice your interest and leave you wanting more, and if I succeed perhaps you'll consider taking a short course on Gestalt or facilitation, or both. (There is probably an iGold program starting soon! And there are other options in the Resources page at the end of this book.) The insights I share are drawn from a variety sources I've stumbled upon during my three decades of practice as a facilitator and consultant.

# IMPACT

Gestalt is still a niche specialty, but facilitation is everywhere. Nearly every leader must know how to lead a meeting, frame a topic, encourage discussion and debate, and help a group move towards resolution. In the Washington, DC region alone (where I live and practice), there are almost 100,000 individual LinkedIn profiles that use the word "facilitate" – and more than three million all together in the United States.

You may be already playing the role of facilitator without realizing it. If you lead a team as part of your job, then you're a facilitator. If you convene Zoom calls for yourself and colleagues, you're facilitating. If you find yourself speaking up in a meeting to help colleagues stay on topic, clarify the question at hand, push for resolution, or just end on time, you're playing the role of a facilitator.

Facilitators emerge in most social groups too. They're the ones who help a quiet family member be heard during a raucous conversation, or enable friends to agree on what movie to watch. We all need people in our lives who step forward at moments of confusion, conflict, or indecision and make it easier for us to do what we have to do.

I use many labels to describe myself, and in this book I've applied several terms interchangeably. When I write about *interveners*, *consultants*, *facilitators*, *practitioners*, *Gestalt-practitioners*, *leaders*, and even *Gestaltists*, I'm thinking of myself...and you the reader. And since facilitation, coaching, and organizational development are merely variations on the same profession (more about this in Chapter 1), you'll also see me refer to *facilitators*, *coaches*, and *OD consultants*, switching up the terms just for variety. I see all of the terms as exchangeable because the insights here can apply to anyone who wants to do better as a family member, friend, spouse, executive, boss, employee, teammate, consultant, or volunteer.

Regardless of the labels that you choose to describe yourself, I invite you to see this book as a resource. I hope it can be of service to you in your journey, wherever it takes you.

# Introduction

Every month or so, I meet with a small group of colleagues who have similar careers as facilitators and coaches and have been trained in Gestalt. We use these informal Community of Practice meetings to talk about our projects and clients, and to stay connected. While we collectively share more than eighty years in our professions, we spend a major portion of our time together thinking about the principles of Gestalt and how we can apply them more effectively in our work. We are striving to have more impact.

Each of us in the Gestalt Community of Practice already believe we're good at our jobs and provide excellent value. And yet we're all looking for ways to become even better, in part by more consistently incorporating Gestalt principles into our practices. Our awkward shorthand for this ambition is that we're "trying to be more Gestalt-y."

# IMPACT

That aspiration, I believe, is based on a couple of underlying premises: Each of us has seen the ways Gestalt can be a powerful and transformative tool in our interactions with others. And we each utilize a mix of principles, habits, and approaches that could be thought of as both "pre-Gestalt" and Gestalt, a mélange of ideas and attitudes that came from a wide range of sources. And to be fair: Gestalt has some slippery premises that are counter-intuitive and a little hard to square with existing perceptions of the world.

So the result is that none of us employs a pure and distilled version of Gestalt. And that's OK, because Gestalt isn't a rigid set of rules that must be adhered to with Talmudic precision.

I have noticed some constants. As Gestalt practitioners, we

- Focus on establishing a compelling and supporting presence
- Collect sensory data and selectively share it
- Make note of patterns, themes, and meanings that emerge (or don't)
- Acknowledge that any intervener becomes part of the system, even when only serving as a short-term consultant
- Accept the significance of ambiguity and paradox
- Express curiosity as a way to generate data and track the flow of energy, interest, and excitement
- Illuminate hidden issues that can impede the ability to change; and
- Facilitate closure and withdrawal at the end of a project.

But that's just a list – and a somewhat opaque one at that. Here's an even more basic description of what Gestaltists do: We raise awareness to mobilize energy for change. You'll read variations on this phrase repeatedly throughout this book, so you might as well underline it, or star it, or highlight it in yellow. If you walk away with just one concept about Gestalt, this would be a good one to hold onto.

# IMPACT

I'll repeat it for emphasis: Gestaltists raise awareness to mobilize energy for change.

I sometimes find myself reflecting on Gestalt's principles during the course of my work, usually when I feel stuck. At times I'll feel bored when talking with a client, and I'll wonder if my reaction is because the topic has slipped away from the "here and now." Or I'll sense that a group feels chaotic and messy, and I'll reflect on whether it's because they're rushing through part of the Cycle of Experience. Some days I'll feel confused when crafting an agenda, and then move forward by better defining the difference between the figure and the ground.

I'll do the same in personal interactions. When a friend makes a presumption about an acquaintance, I'll think about how she's managing her boundaries. When a colleague is exhausted after starting multiple projects without finishing any, I'll reflect on the Unit of Work. When a cousin refuses to discuss a long-simmering family slight, I'll think about how pain and resistance can color relationships and how we interact with others.

Years after my first Gestalt training, I'm getting better at reaching into my mental Gestalt bag and pulling out a tool for the challenge in front of me. And when I get the opportunity to work with a Gestalt-trained colleague, I can see the different ways a person might use those mental models to support their work.

This makes me Gestalt practitioner, but not an expert. I still have habits of mind that pre-date my Gestalt training, and although I'm practicing and learning (and writing a book about Gestalt!), some of its principles remain a little dense and confusing to me. I'm on a journey to become more Gestalt-y, but I still haven't arrived.

I will never become a Gestalt expert or scholar. And yet, here I am evangelizing about Gestalt because I've come to see how impactful it is, particularly when paired with the ideas and approaches that I've learned as a facilitator.

Gestalt has been characterized by its own practitioners as "the indescribable experience." When it works, it can look and feel like magic. Its effectiveness is difficult to explain and sometimes hard to believe. And even more confounding: When it doesn't work as planned, it can still transcend expectations and defy explanation.

While facilitation's tenets are easier to grasp, I encourage you to consider the value of both the simple facilitation techniques I'll describe, as well as the squishier, more evanescent Gestalt concepts. Don't worry if it all doesn't make perfect sense; some sections or paragraphs may merit a second or third reading, perhaps right away or sometime in the future. Some things will land and others won't.

This is a short book (with illustrations!), so don't get dissuaded. Keep going. As you read and reflect, you might find a small "aha" in an unexpected place, leading to new ways for you to be even more present, powerful, and impactful.

# IMPACT

# Part 1: The Beginning

*"The beginning is the
most important part of the work."*

Plato

# Chapter 1

## Impact

Author Daniel Pink has pointed out that for most of human history people worked primarily to avoid deprivation, keeping themselves fed, housed, and safe. To the extent they achieved those basic aims, their lives could be thought of as a success.

Today, millions of middle-class people around the world are in a far more privileged place: While we might have hard times or financial struggles, we generally don't work to avoid deprivation. Most of us have the privilege to work with the goal of finding meaning.

My friends at the Sierra Club find meaning by combating climate change. My acquaintances at Planned Parenthood defend women's rights. My friends at the ACLU fight to support people's right to vote.

But meaning is not just for the socially and politically active. Two colleagues quit their corporate jobs to open a coffee shop because they find meaning in the small pleasure of a well-baked scone. Some, like me, find meaning in helping organizations collaborate and communicate more effectively.

Our aspirations come in all shapes and sizes. Some seek meaning at the interpersonal or intrapersonal level. Organizational development consultants may help create meaning across a community. My Sierra Club colleagues and others are driven to work on a global scale.

In all these cases, meaning comes from making an impact, knowing that our presence made a difference. We strive to find the role where our contribution matters.

As I noted in the Preface, I had felt ineffectual in my work as a political consultant. What I really wanted was to help, and to be a catalyst for success. I wanted to make a difference, even if it was on a small scale.

I found my meaning in facilitation, a job that literally means "to make easier." Making meetings and other processes easier is a way for me to be of service to others, and to have an impact…even though the value of what I do can be difficult to quantify.

Partly, this is my own doing: Clients hire me to achieve an outcome, but I have found my greatest gifts are around providing a process, an approach, a safe space, and a willingness to adapt to the moment. I have come to realize I can make a bigger impact not by fixating on bottom-line results, but by affecting the ways things get done. I give attention to achieving the outcomes my clients seek, but I hold those goals more lightly than they do. Paradoxically, this makes my impact on their outcomes even greater.

The results speak for themselves. Since integrating Gestalt into my practice, I have become an "award winning facilitator!"

My work was recognized as among the most impactful in the world in 2020 and 2021 as the back-to-back recipient of the Platinum Facilitation Impact Award, the International Association of Facilitators' highest honor. I received one award for my work with the Child Neurology Foundation.

# IMPACT

In 2021, I was part of a team with two of my Gestalt colleagues, Michael Randel and Heather Berthoud, supporting the SD Bechtel, Jr. Foundation.

My Gestalt training has helped me see that my impact is less about the thing I happen to be doing, and more about how I am when I'm doing it. It's the data I sense and the data I overlook. It's how and when I choose to step forward, when I hold back (which is, paradoxically, also an intervention), and the intention I hold when I'm doing it.

Lots of other facilitators don't see it that way. One of the largest facilitation training programs, the oddly-named Technology of Participation (ToP), focuses on teaching a long list of battle-tested activities such as ice-breakers, energizers, brainstorming, dot voting, and other methods. Most of the books and trainings that teach facilitation (some by ToP practitioners) tend to be similarly formulaic, with detailed activities that anyone can replicate. And that's not nothing: Being able to lead an engaging exercise can save an otherwise boring meeting, and help a group get its work done.

But with their excessive attention to methodology, activities, and outcomes, my ToP-trained colleagues end up learning the text of facilitation without ever grasping its poetry or music. Perhaps this provides enough impact and meaning for them. It's not enough for me.

I've found the sweet spot by becoming more Gestalt-y, and less like those ToP practitioners, or ToP-y. Over the course of the upcoming chapters, I'll explain how many of these concepts can help you elevate your impact as well.

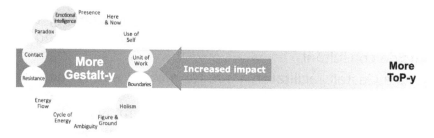

I would never have been a great ToP practitioner anyway, because I have never been able to hold a deep catalogue of facilitation methods in my head. At times, my poor memory has come back to bite me. Seeking to be recognized as a Certified Professional Facilitator by the International Association of Facilitators in 2000, I was asked to name a few processes I had found effective over the course of my practice. In response, I came up blank. So I rambled, realizing that I had no idea what even the most basic collaboration tools were called – even though I had used them for years.

Fortunately, I have always had other gifts as a facilitator. I excel at framing questions, creating a playful and inviting atmosphere, zeroing-in on details, pulling back to see the big picture, and improvising methods on the fly. Apparently, I showed enough dexterity on that IAF testing day to demonstrate my impact. Despite my floundering, I received my CPF certification and have maintained it ever since.

Gestalt has helped me redefine my role. In my early years, clients would ask me to help their group accomplish a relatively straightforward task, like "Help us develop a plan for the coming year," and I would try to do so without much forethought. I rarely concerned myself with whether the task made sense, or if it was meaningful.

I was uninterested in whether the group was well-equipped to make informed choices during our meeting or take the requisite actions after they were agreed. And I never inquired into the kinds of resistance that existed in the organization, resistance which had made the simple tasks of convening and strategizing so challenging that they couldn't figure out how to proceed without hiring an outside consultant.

As a Gestalt facilitator, I aim for more. I aim to mobilize others' energy for change by raising awareness and noticing "what is," holding optimism, ambivalence, and ambiguity with patience, and using myself as an instrument of change. I don't just help clients complete tasks; I help them learn to be more effective, powerful, and resilient. I aim to get the work done, and help the group change for the better in the process.

One way I do this is by holding a balance between what I call "transactionalism" on one hand, and what is known in Gestalt as "contact" on the other. Both terms merit a little unpacking.

Transactionalism is the attention one might devote to the basic transactions of the day. Making one's breakfast is a transaction. Scheduling a Zoom call is a transaction. Writing a report is a transaction, and so is responding to each of those pesky emails.

My ex-boyfriend was the King of Transactionalism. He would arrive at his desk each morning for his job as an architect and write an astonishingly detailed To Do list for himself. As the day would progress, he'd check the little "Completed" boxes next to each item, and then move on to the next. At the end of the day, he'd evaluate his success by reviewing the number of boxes he had ticked.

Weekends were the same. On Saturday morning, I'd awake to a list of Honey-Do chores. Seeing it always made my heart sink.

# IMPACT

Paying attention to transactions is critical, of course. Jobs have duties that must be accomplished...and once you get home the trash must be brought to the curb. Things must be done; transactions must be completed.

On the other end of the continuum is the Gestalt concept of "contact," which can be thought of as the moment when a more profound kind of change takes place, usually inside a person or between individuals. Contact is the sudden "a-ha" that reframes a situation or redefines a relationship.

Contact is the moment when "the scales fall from your eyes," and you can suddenly see a situation clearly and accurately. Contact is when you realize the truth about something (or someone...or yourself) after not having been able to perceive it with clarity and coherence.

Gestaltists know that contact is a critical step towards transformation. For lasting change to happen in an organization or an individual, there must first be contact.

But it's very bad form to go around forcing people to confront hidden truths about themselves or one another. Each of us keeps a batch of "truths" hidden all the time for a myriad of good (and not so good) reasons.

And besides: Our friends, colleagues, and consultants probably didn't sign up for therapy. Most of us get paid to do the work at hand, not blithely root around in the dark recesses of other people's emotions and psyches.

So it makes sense to hold a space in our professional and social realms for both transactionalism and contact to take place. In my work, I structure my interactions with clients around the purpose of completing tasks, while simultaneously remaining alert for moments where contact might be helpful.

It's a delicate balance. Too much contact can be overwhelming and exhausting. Too little contact can result in lots of tasks completed and boxes checked, but with groups and individuals lacking the ability to do anything differently. The result is that the disappointing results of the past are more likely to be repeated over and over again into the future.

# IMPACT

While Gestalt may be indescribable, facilitation itself isn't as neat a concept as I once believed either. It isn't just standing in front of a room of twenty people (or convening a group on Zoom) in the typical facilitator mode, yellow stickies, flip charts, and magic markers at the ready. A facilitator can also be a coach or an organizational development consultant, or both, since the boundaries between these three disciplines is less clear-cut than I had once imagined.

All three sit along a continuum. On one end is coaching, in which the consultant may work with a single person at a time helping raise awareness of patterns of behavior and relationships, mobilize energy, and help the individual develop strategies to make a change. A coach can also support a pair of people or small group, helping them develop new insights about their inter-relationships. Individuals and small groups often turn to coaching at times of transition, when starting new responsibilities, when past strategies aren't working like they used to, or when it's time to confront a simmering challenge.

In the middle of the continuum is facilitation, in which the practitioner supports collaboration and communication within a specific group – often a department, division, or team. Facilitators also convene multiple organizations (a specialty of mine), bringing together peers within a sector to explore a shared challenge. Usually, the outcome for such meetings is some sort of collective action among the various groups.

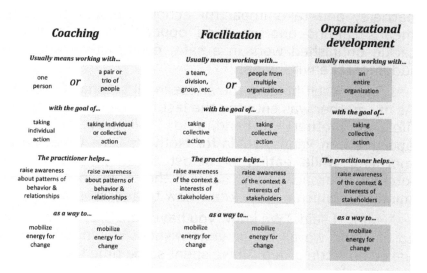

At the farthest end of the continuum is organizational development, when an entire organization is attempting to do something new or do something differently. Some consultants call this "change management." When I take on such projects, facilitation and coaching are always key components because I've found those are the most effective ways to raise awareness, mobilize energy, and support change.

My practice includes coaching, facilitation, and OD. As I mentioned earlier, I market this as "helping groups and individuals communicate and collaborate." In many cases, that really means "helping people get unstuck."

Individuals who are stuck in unproductive patterns of behavior may seek out a coach to help break those patterns. Groups and teams may be stuck in old habits or mindsets, or too focused on the grind of their day-to-day responsibilities to see the bigger picture. Some problems faced by organizations or teams may seem too big and complex to tackle because emotions are high, because critical information is compartmentalized, or because there is a history of failure.

In each case, it's the facilitator's job to "hold the space" for participants to strip away confusion, to see things as they really are, address unfinished business, overcome barriers, and take impactful action. Holding the space means carving out time and opportunity for people to tackle unfinished work in a safe, constructive, and non-judgmental environment.

I find myself holding the space in all settings of my life. As my mother was entering the last few months of her long life, my brother, husband, and I all drove up to her apartment in Pennsylvania for Mother's Day. On Saturday morning, while eating breakfast together in her small kitchen, I broached the subject that was on everyone's mind...but which no one knew how to address.

"Mom," I said. "We know you have said that you're ready to die, and we all honor your wishes. Would it be ok," I asked our little group, "if we spent some time talking about that now?"

There was silence. My brother looked down at his bowl of breakfast cereal. My husband fidgeted with his English muffin.

My mother looked up without a hint of emotion. "Yes," she said firmly, and my brother and husband silently agreed.

In that moment we became unstuck, finally able to have the long-delayed conversation we needed to have. We told her that she should feel free to let herself die whenever the time comes, that we didn't want her to hold onto life just to protect us from pain. We said we'd be very sad, but we'd be OK. She said she heard us and loved us. We ended with a family embrace.

In a professional setting, the role of "holding the space" is more formalized. I'll propose an agenda and boundaries that support everyone's participation and enable all stakeholders to work on the same things at the same time. I'll welcome both disagreement and alignment, and after enough time has elapsed, I'll bring the process to a close. I see myself as the steward of fairness and access, and a catalyst for change.

My contributions aren't always welcome. One international organization is notorious for getting cold feet in the middle of work they've hired me to do. In one case, I crafted an agenda with the client's guidance that would challenge the team to do things a little differently. My approach was meant to help them break out of their self-described pattern of making plans but failing to follow-through, and my approach received the enthusiastic blessing of the planning team and their senior vice president.

Then they flew me from Washington, DC to Vienna, Austria to facilitate a session they had touted as "something different" and "transformative." But after just a few hours of meeting together, the vice president heard pushback from senior staff members who had long benefitted from the old ways of doing things. She quickly folded. She tossed aside my agenda and relegated me to the back of the room while she reasserted control to run a "traditional" meeting. With nothing to do, I played a lot of Tetris on my phone that day.

Occasionally I encounter pushback in my personal life too. My ex once rebuked me in the middle of an argument, demanding with exasperation, "Don't facilitate me!!"

When it goes well (which honestly, is 99% of the time), the role of facilitator places me paradoxically both "front and center" and also on the periphery. It's a challenge to keep those two postures in proper balance.

Not every facilitator succeeds in every situation. For example, we all know leaders who love the sound of their own voices, and who feel the need to reflect on every comment and decide every question. When working with such a person, we may be blinded by their charisma and charm, but their behavior severely limits the time and attention that's available for everyone else. They put themselves so much at the center that they are less like facilitators and more like autocrats, where all things of value must pass first through their filters before they can be accepted as valid.

The best practitioners are fully present without demanding to be the center of attention. Rather than using the role to feed one's narcissism, the effective facilitator is curious about others, curious about what is happening, and curious what might happen next. We don't force resolution or control events. We support exploration, abide confusion, and sit with ambiguity as way to help others fulfill their potential.

Most non-facilitator consultants see their role differently. They stake their value on what they know and can impart to others. They sell their ability to tell, explain, direct, solve, and do. They enter the client relationship in the hopes of looking smart and providing rock-solid answers.

In contrast, there is an ambivalent modesty to the facilitator's role. As a facilitator, I know I am a vital presence yet I see myself as more supportive than central. This doesn't mean I don't have an ego. On the contrary: When I'm "in the zone" I feel irreplaceable, and that honestly makes me feel amazing.

I try to model myself after a baseball umpire, who serves a critical but somewhat invisible role. Baseball games can't function without umpires, but those officials are never the most important actors on the field. It's the players who hit the home runs and throw the strikes, and it's their skills and accomplishments that carry the game forward. When the umpires do their jobs correctly everyone remembers what the players did, while barely recalling that the umpires were even on the field.

Many ToP-trained facilitators tend to focus on offering a range of tasks and exercises for participants to complete. One snarky colleague referred to their meetings as "adult preschool," full of fun, engaging, but relatively pointless activities meant to keep hands busy and eat up time.

As a Gestalt-trained facilitator, I aspire to be not just fun, challenging, and dispassionate, but to also topple barriers that might inhibit any person's full involvement. This is never simple. Every organization carries the burden of both invisible and visible structures that place some people at high status and others at a lower status. Such dynamics have myriad pernicious effects.

And those barriers are everywhere. Every individual is implicated, myself included. I'm a 21st century American, so patriarchy, homophobia, tribalism, fat-phobia, racism and untold other biases have been present in my environment since birth, and they are therefore present in me. Like microplastics in the food chain, these noxious elements have been in my air and water, and now they are part of my fiber. I really, really don't like it, but I have to accept this is true. All those "isms" that push people down, degrade our community, and tear at the fabric of society are part of my cultural DNA.

So try as I might to be fair, loving, and welcoming, I can't always discern the ways my actions and presence as a white, middle-class, college-educated English-speaking cis-male might contribute to others' feelings of being unwelcome, unseen, or unheard.

I am always grateful to be reminded about how differently well-meaning and capable adults can experience the exact same situations. Here's an example: My male-led consulting team met with our client to provide a short presentation, which we delivered off-the-cuff without notes, visuals, or documentation. The following week, a separate female-led consulting team did roughly the same thing, but their presentation was tightly scripted and organized, and supported by a sharp-looking PowerPoint.

Was there meaning to these different approaches? A colleague speculated that the contrast could be emblematic of the ways women and men have been acculturated to handle challenging career moments. The women, guarding against not being taken seriously, were methodical, efficient, comprehensive, and left nothing to chance. The men, confident that we would be recognized as serious, were loose and self-assured to the point of being almost lackadaisical in our preparations.

In another example, a colleague described a fraught interaction with her boss who had criticized her for being an unwelcome "feminist" in the workplace. My exasperated peer saw this as yet another example of how black women are always expected to be compliant and nonconfrontational, even by other women. As she put it, "I'm not sure what a 'feminist' is, I just know I only get called a 'feminist' when I differentiate myself from a doormat."

I suspect that a man would have been less likely to be subject to such a ham-handed and personal critique. (And it was such an odd sort of slam: Is "feminist" even a put-down in 2024?)

I hear often about the difficult path women must tread in the professional world (especially women of color) between expressions of strength and power that are considered appropriate for men, and the traditional expectations that women must be nurturing, accommodating to the point of acquiescence, and dependent. It makes my head spin to be writing this, but since these anachronistic attitudes continue to persist they must be consistently recognized and addressed.

Racism, sexism, homophobia, and other social cancers continue to color our interactions and push people apart. Gestalt facilitators must step into that space with our eyes and our hearts wide open, with the courage to confront the darkest parts of our culture when they diminish individuals and groups. We continually seek ways to celebrate difference, acknowledge our own imperfections, and provide safety and support for every person in the system.

## One foot in, one foot out

More than prioritizing methods, the best facilitators pay attention to their own stance, approaching the work with a mixture of compassion, optimism, and modesty. This starts by metaphorically positioning oneself with one foot in the group, and one foot outside the group. The inside foot enables us to see what's happening, understand the conversation, and read the emotional signals of others. The foot outside the group enables us to keep our eye on the process, to assess whether the group is on or off-track, and invite outside perspectives that might support the work.

Some practitioners lean heavily on the foot that's inside the group. In doing so, they may become, as my colleague

Heather Berthoud says, "seduced by the content," getting so engaged by the ideas expressed by participants that they are drawn deeply into the fray, thereby losing a measure of their effectiveness.

This is especially problematic for someone who is already a member of the group, knows a lot about the topic being discussed, and/or may have opinions about what should be done. Facilitators who are too close or too knowledgeable can lose their impartiality and diminish their value.

Such a confluent facilitator may struggle in other ways, being unwilling to challenge existing norms of behavior even when those patterns clearly undermine the group's goals. In other cases, one may try to keep people happy by withholding challenging ideas or feedback. Or the facilitator may depend excessively on charisma and charm, bringing so much attention to her/himself that the group's needs get subordinated.

The facilitator has to be connected enough in the moment to make sense of what's going on and to be accepted. And sure: It can be fun and reassuring as the facilitator to feel in-sync with participants. But what makes you truly valuable as a facilitator is the foot that's outside the group. The ways in which you are different enable you to bring something unique, something that's missing, to the situation that otherwise would not be present.

Over-emphasizing either foot is problematic, as brilliantly captured in Jonno Hanafin's "Perceived Weirdness Index." On one side of the scale is a facilitator who is perceived as excessively weird or different. Such a presence will be useless, because the group will tend to reject that person and anything he or she might contribute.

On the other side of Hanafin's scale is the facilitator who is so confluent and similar to those who are already there that they add nothing new. Such a person is easy for others to accept...but why would the group need another person who is exactly like everyone else who's already there?

# IMPACT

## Perceived Weirdness Index

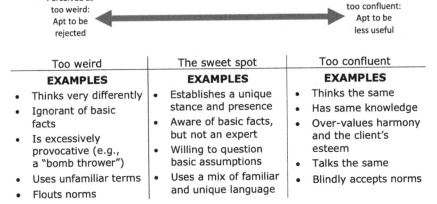

| Too weird | The sweet spot | Too confluent |
|---|---|---|
| **EXAMPLES** | **EXAMPLES** | **EXAMPLES** |
| • Thinks very differently | • Establishes a unique stance and presence | • Thinks the same |
| • Ignorant of basic facts | • Aware of basic facts, but not an expert | • Has same knowledge |
| • Is excessively provocative (e.g., a "bomb thrower") | • Willing to question basic assumptions | • Over-values harmony and the client's esteem |
| • Uses unfamiliar terms | • Uses a mix of familiar and unique language | • Talks the same |
| • Flouts norms | | • Blindly accepts norms |

Credit: Jonno Hanafin

When I started consulting at the Pentagon twenty years ago, I panicked that the macho military bros might reject me outright as a sissified city boy with nothing of value to offer. I had a story in my head (based on my own insecurities) that these officers would treat me like the school bus bullies I had encountered in junior high school. I was afraid they'd steal my lunch money and toss my books out the window.

I was thrilled to find out that the opposite was true. The military personnel and civilians quickly saw my differences of style and approach as interesting and valuable, rather than disqualifying. They embraced me as a difference-maker who would help them achieve their single-minded goal, which was to fulfill their mission.

So the task for any facilitator (but especially a Gestaltist) is to find the sweet spot in the middle. One must cultivate a measured degree of uniqueness that keeps people interested and curious, but not flaunt your differences so much as to cause revulsion and rejection. Striking the right balance allows you to win others' interest and trust without seeming like just another drone in the hive.

Note that Hanafin isn't warning about *being* weird or confluent; the focus here is on being *perceived* as too weird or confluent in the eyes of others. It's those unproductive perceptions that will affect your ability to be influential.

It can be difficult to maintain the appropriate balance of differentness and sameness so one can be perceived as productively weird. Several years ago, after many years of consulting for FM Global, a multinational insurance company, I was approached by a senior executive I had never met before, a gregarious bear of a man who wanted my help in understanding some troubling dynamics in his division.

With his agreement, I conducted confidential individual and small-group interviews with a wide variety of his employees. Throughout my inquiry, I heard consistent themes about bullying behavior and consistent intolerance of contrary views from the highest levels of the division. At the end of the process, I organized my data and met with the boss to let him know what I had learned.

Perhaps I should have guessed what would happen next. As I started to share feedback from his staff, his mood quickly changed from kindly to belligerent. Instead of seeing me as an ally, he began to see me as a foreign invader. He charged that I "didn't understand" the company, and that I had misconstrued or willfully misrepresented what I had been told by his staff. His tone became curt and angry, and I was at a loss for how to defend myself.

After the confrontational exchange in the office, we broke for dinner at a fancy restaurant, where he continued to loudly belittle me and my work in front of his lieutenants and within earshot of other customers. I felt like a whipped puppy. I managed to make it through the dinner and hang on until my contract was completed, but shortly thereafter he severed all contact with me. He couldn't wait to get me out of his hair...and I couldn't wait to be done with him either.

From today's vantage point I can see that my client rejected me because I had inadvertently broken an unwritten rule within his division; I had given voice to the disgruntled views of his subordinates. I had said to his face what everyone was saying behind his back, and this was not OK.

True, he asked me to conduct the inquiry. And he agreed to the process I used to collect the data that he so roundly rejected.

In retrospect, I might have appreciated how explosive my information was, and paid more attention to the underlying lesson his employees were sharing with me. When they delivered bad news to him it was only in small bites, and they wrapped each bitter pill in the honey of good news and compliments. They became extremely confluent with the boss as a way to survive his rages.

This careful approach never occurred to me. I foolishly believed that since the boss was paying me to tell him unvarnished truths I should do just that, regardless of how harsh that might feel. I naively said the things that everyone in the division knew but had learned to keep to themselves.

As a result, he perceived me as far too "weird" to keep around. As soon as he discovered my differentness, he kicked me out of the system.

## Use of Self

My Gestalt training has enabled me to use more of myself in my work, and to see myself clearly as an instrument of change. Before, I used my intellect and personality to support my clients, but I generally overlooked the flood of other data that was available to me. Gestalt has taught me that the sensations in my body are data, as is my awareness of those sensations. The meaning I make of those sensations is data, and so are the actions I may take as a result.

The different approaches can lead to very different results. During our iGold class in Amsterdam, our teacher John Nkum told us about his strategic planning work with a large construction firm. After weeks of interviewing staff to understand the company's dynamics, several members of John's team began feel physically ill, as if they had contracted food poisoning.

Did this emerging pattern have any significance to their work, or not? Who knows? Maybe the mayonnaise on the corporate salad bar had been sitting out just a little too long.

The consulting team soon discovered that a subset of employees in the company had been experiencing similar symptoms for years. As executives rose through the corporate ranks, they often began to suffer chronic indigestion and higher-than-normal rates of absenteeism. Junior staff and support personnel, in contrast, reported no such problems.

It wasn't the mayonnaise. John hypothesized that there was something about the toxic work environment that had made its leaders ill. By paying attention to the data coming from their own bodies, the consulting team revealed a pattern that shifted their focus. Only then were they able to explore the most significant issues that had been driving the company's distress.

In the same way, I now constantly monitor my own body and emotions when I work. I've come to learn that if I'm bored, other people may also be bored. When I feel my energy wane, I begin to wonder if others are also checking out. And when I notice a knot in my gut, or my skin growing flush, or my fingers getting tingly...I wonder what's happening inside of me and what, if anything, it might mean for the people around me.

Before my Gestalt training, I habitually set such data aside because I thought it was an irrelevant distraction. Now I try to take Fritz Perl's advice to "lose your mind and come to your senses." As a Gestalt facilitator, I now know I am part of the client's system for as long as I'm there. What's going on with my mind, body, and emotions are all relevant.

Relevant, yes...but maybe not meaningful. The Gestalt practitioner must be guided not only by self-knowledge, but also by humility. I can't presume that others are feeling the same way. It's possible it is just me.

So, are those sensations I'm feeling significant or not? It pays to know your own patterns.

As I noted earlier, I started this part of my career as a support group facilitator, so I get incredibly excited whenever a group shifts their attention from the cognitive realm of facts and ideas to more visceral and emotional topics. It feels important and valuable when participants get below the surface, open themselves up to the emotions and values that animate them, bring their discomforts to light, and get real. Over the years, I've been thrilled to support people digging deeper to have difficult, transformative conversations.

But as I was reminded recently, my emotional needs don't always align with the needs of others. For several months I had been facilitating a peer group of evaluators working for national youth service organizations. Those conversations were warm, but superficial. Participants talked about the challenges of their job, and shared ideas for addressing data collection dilemmas and personnel issues.

At one of our quarterly meetings, the conversation swerved suddenly into the painful legacy of child abuse in the youth development sector. Although the people in the room had no direct connection to the tragic stories that had made international headlines, several participants tearfully described their shame and guilt about working for organizations that had demonstrated indifference (or worse) in the face of these horrifying crimes. It was a fascinating and emotional moment.

As the discussion grew darker and more personal, several speakers started expressing their feelings more directly. Eyes became red, and voices cracked with emotion. I found myself leaning forward in my seat, my attention becoming sharper. I encouraged participants to dig deep and continue to share whatever they were experiencing. For my part, I felt excited and grateful to see them grappling with profound topics that had been lurking below the surface all along.

After a while we took a break, and when we re-gathered a participant announced without explanation that one member would not return for the rest of the day. We noted her absence and continued with our work, moving from heavy emotional topics to the more mundane conversations we had typically held.

The next morning I learned that the participant who excused herself had herself been the victim of child sex abuse, and that she felt triggered by the conversation we experienced together. The news filled me with shame and remorse.

I had become so excited about my own desire to explore these emotional topics that I failed to notice the pained expression on the woman sitting right next to me. I had encouraged a conversation that felt meaningful and productive without weighing its potential to do harm. In doing so, I served some people's interests (most pointedly, my own) and ignored the needs of others.

In retrospect, I might have moved more slowly and with more intention in that moment. As the conversation delved into a deeper and more personal realm, I might have noticed my personal enthusiasm for the topic, and then checked to see whether others were feeling the same. Instead of simply reveling in my own excitement, I could have looked around to room to observe the signals being sent by others.

I don't know what I would have observed; perhaps nothing would have been obvious to me. I do recall that many people were looking down or fiddling with their hands, and there were many moist eyes, including my own.

At minimum, I could have leaned on my foot outside the circle. I might have mentioned my perception that this level of discourse was different from the group's usual conversation, and then waited to see what would happen. I might have invited participants to say how they felt about the change in tone and content, and then we could have worked together to decide on how to proceed.

This story is a reminder to me to continually check-in with myself when I am with my clients, to remain aware of what I'm experiencing, and to remain curious about what they're experiencing too. The challenge for any facilitator is to hold all those emotions and desires in the proper balance, and then act with both modesty and intention.

## Leadership

Gestalt-trained professionals are leaders, whether we sit at a traditional place atop an organizational chart, enter a conversation as a consultant, or act merely as an observer. But what does it mean to be a leader? Our culture's concept of effective leadership has changed dramatically over time. American culture used to venerate just one leadership archetype – the Great Man – but today leaders must show up differently than in the past.

The leader's job now is to create and maintain a culture, to share power, elevate the needs of employees, and help them develop and perform as effectively as possible. This model, sometimes called Empathetic Leadership or Servant Leadership, flips the autocratic Great Man on his stony gray head.

Empathetic leaders are secure in their prominence, acknowledging that their leadership status automatically makes them the center of attention among the people they supervise. Since they command attention as the default, there's no need for them to bark orders or make flamboyant displays of dominance.

Working from this baseline, the most effective leaders deliver quiet signals based on shared goals and values, and create emotional resonance with those around them. They hold genuine curiosity about others' experiences, and how changes in the environment might feel. They join their colleagues in both the tactical and emotional space, sharing the challenges of operating in a chaotic world.

And this is an especially chaotic time. The COVID pandemic and resulting disruptions have called into question a lot of our perceptions, opinions, beliefs, and attitudes about work and personal life. Leaders and managers with whom I speak are more confused than ever by the expectations of their employees, especially the younger ones.

Even though what they hear may be confusing, the best leaders continually collect data from their employees. Leaders remove barriers and provide resources, create air cover for errors, and carve out safe zones where individuals can let their guard down. In return, team members are confident they won't be undervalued, sidelined, or punished for speaking up.

In a way, today's leaders are selfless facilitators. They model curiosity in service of the organizational mission and the team. Rather than trying to chalk up wins and losses on some cosmic scoreboard, work is framed as a learning dilemma, a journey of discovery that has no interest in cataloguing right or wrong answers. Such leaders strive for synergy rather than obedience.

Today's employees and allies demand nothing less. We expect authenticity, empathy, care, flexibility, and transparency. When we fail to get what we need from our leaders, we rebel.

When I think of leaders with whom I've worked, I am reminded of this great Maya Angelou quote: "At the end of the day people won't remember what you said or did. They will remember how you made them feel." My best bosses made me feel confident and empowered. My worst bosses made me feel uncertain, incapable, and anxious.

Not every Gestaltist holds an explicit leadership title, but because we share many of the same values and approaches we naturally align with Servant or Empathetic Leaders. We share curiosity about people, their patterns of behavior, their emotions and relationships, and their energy. We use our influence to raise awareness, so individuals and groups can overcome barriers and move ahead. Even when they struggle, we celebrate our colleagues as whole, powerful, and capable. Like other Empathetic Leaders, Gestalt practitioners listen to ourselves and listen to others, and act with intention.

## Patience and resilience

Paying attention to my own sensations when I'm facilitating a meeting generates a lot of data. I might notice the energy in the room and the physical cues being shown by participants; it's a lot of data to sort through! Listening to the content of a conversation, thinking about how long it will be before the next break, and measuring the work to be accomplished against the time remaining in the meeting – all of that produces a lot of data too. It can be overwhelming!

Jonno Hanafin likens the facilitator in such moments to a duck. On the surface, the duck appears to be gliding serenely across the lake. What you can't see is the frantic action down below, where the duck is paddling furiously.

Gestalt interveners can often find ourselves paddling with enormous fervor. Once I started to notice more data during my facilitation gigs, I wasn't sure what deserved attention and what could be set aside. In many cases, I felt compelled to act on what I was observing...which didn't leave room for participants to do their work. So I realized that in addition to attention, I needed to cultivate my patience and compassion.

The facilitator needs patience because everything doesn't need to be addressed as soon as it's noticed. If the energy in a meeting is low, that might be OK. If someone is feeling and expressing strong emotions, that might be OK. If the group is confused or frustrated, that might be OK.

My job isn't to alleviate all pain while assuring maximum efficiency. It is to facilitate beneficial change in a way that protects people from lasting injury. Doing so requires me to maintain a delicate and uncertain balance. I am continually weighing when to step in and when to hold back, considering what kind of intervention will best serve the long-term interests of the client.

And in choosing which steps to take and when, the outcomes won't always be clean and tidy. The low energy I notice in a meeting might linger longer than I would like and can drag the whole process down. The person in front of me who is experiencing strong emotions might get overwhelmed, or the display may sidetrack others. Conversations can go into the weeds and get tangled. A confused or frustrated group can lose its focus.

This is where personal resilience comes in: Even the best and most experienced practitioners will fail to act effectively in a fraught moment or choose an intervention that doesn't work out as planned, so one must be ready to set that aside and move forward with confidence. Jazz legend Miles Davis has said, "There's no such thing as a wrong note." He's right. It doesn't matter whether any specific intervention works out as hoped; what matters is what you do next.

You might notice that patience and resilience are two recurring themes in this book, and both will be examined again later. Both of these qualities are essential to the Gestalt practice, and they are among the most difficult qualities I struggle to embody. If fact, I confess to being preternaturally impatient. I'm always ready to move on to the next thing as soon as whatever I'm doing seems about 75% complete. I've lost interest in the last several items on every To Do list I've ever created.

So although I preach resilience for individuals and organizations, I feel I rarely exemplify it myself. I am frequently sidetracked by petty frustrations, disappointments, and poor personal planning.

Yes, you might find it a bit ironic that such a self-described impatient and non-resilient person is preaching the concepts of patience and resilience. But there is an upside: Since I'm so often irritated with myself when I fall short, I continually re-examine my behaviors in hopes of minimizing the damaging impacts. The result is that I am well-attuned to how impatience and non-resilience look in myself and others.

## Ambiguity and paradox

Here's a bigger personal challenge for me: As a Gestalt practitioner, I have had to accept that ambiguity and paradox are normal circumstances of the human condition. It hasn't been easy.

Like many people, I like things to come to neat resolution. I like knowing the answer. I like a problem to be fixed. When a task finally is complete, I feel a rush of satisfaction, and a sense of contentedness deep in my core. I love it when the puzzle pieces click into place. I like finishing one thing so I can move on to the next.

Sadly, life is rarely that neat. Most questions don't have clear answers, and many projects don't come to a definitive conclusion. Things tend to linger, drift, and peter out.

I can't just blame the outside world for being full of ambiguity. I'm as guilty as anyone of acting in ambiguous ways, mostly by failing to decide or failing to bring simple processes to completion.

It's not just me either. Ambiguity is a feature of the human experience. We demand answers and resolution while we're still collecting data. We ache to be at the finish line when we're just starting the race. We feel incomplete and empty because we ache to feel satisfied and done.

I regularly caution my clients to be on alert for the pain of ambiguity and unsettledness. At the start of a long project, I might forewarn all who will listen: "We'll get to the end of the day today without any answers or clear resolution to the problems you want to solve. This may feel bad to you. You may feel like our time has been wasted or that we will have failed. In fact, it is normal to experience a sense of incompleteness at that point because our work together won't be done. I invite you to notice those feelings of ambiguity and accept them as normal and appropriate."

Ambiguity shows up in other ways too. In the complex environments of our professional and personal lives, it's possible to feel strongly one way about an issue...and also feel strongly in a contradictory direction. For instance, I really enjoyed spending time with my aging mother, but I also found my conversations with her to be irritating and exhausting. (Sorry, mom!) I love my work and hate it at the same time. (Sorry, clients!)

These seemingly opposite truths can and do co-exist. One truth is not cancelled out by its counterpart.

In Gestalt, we notice and accept that all forms and flavors of ambiguity can be normal and appropriate. While unsettling, these are not, by themselves, evidence of disorder or disfunction. We hold all of this – ambiguous attitudes within ourselves and others – with curiosity and compassion.

While ambiguity can be irritating, paradoxes can leave us feeling lost and confused. A paradox is a seemingly absurd or self-contradictory proposition that turns out to be true. In science fiction: A time-traveler goes into the past and kills his mother...which makes it impossible for him to be born and travel back in time to kill his mother. The scoundrel declares, "Everything I say is a lie," so is that statement unreliable too? And what happens exactly when an unstoppable force meets an immovable object?

The paradoxes we encounter in everyday life are far more prosaic, and I detail a few later in this book. For now it is enough to note that Gestalt practitioners hold paradoxes as normal, even as we acknowledge them as baffling.

# Chapter 2

# Self-Knowledge and Presence

As I sketched in Chapter 1, the Gestalt intervener makes note of what they are sensing in themselves as a way to make meaning of what's going on with others. But to do so, one must be able to distinguish between a fair amount of signal and lots and lots of noise.

This is particularly complicated because such "use of self" requires the practitioner to be both the instrument and the evaluator of the instrument. As Robert Penn Warren wrote, "If you look at a thing, the very fact of your looking changes it. If you think about yourself, that very fact changes you." We must be able to see ourselves in the mirror, recognize that it's not really us (It's a reflection!), acknowledge that everything is just a little distorted and backwards, make meaning of all the distortions, and still make a wise choice about how to respond.

Self-knowledge helps the practitioner sort between meaningful data and data that can be set aside – between what's "my shit" and what's "other people's shit." As I've noted, I am aware and upfront about my impatience, and it's not all bad. In optimal moments, I can use those impatient feelings to help a client keep things moving and push towards timely conclusions.

But I also realize that at other times my impatience is just my impatience. Even though I'm ready to move on, it may better serve a client's needs to slow things down, linger in the moment, and delay any hasty action. In this way, self-knowledge has a transactional benefit; it helps me see the environment more clearly and make better sense of the data I perceive, which in turn helps me decide how best to respond.

Self-knowledge leads to presence, the hard-to-define internal gyroscope that acts like a magnet, drawing people's curiosity and attention. And cultivating your presence, as I'll show in a moment, is a powerful way to build your impact.

Presence, however, is a squishy concept because it includes so much. It can be thought of as a compelling integration of everything you are, and everything you are perceived to be – your perceptions, feelings, thoughts, and behaviors. It's your past, your present, and your future. It's your reputation, the way you show up, and the expectations about what's next. Your presence is created by you through circumstance and deliberate choices, but also by others as they reflect back their own reactions and responses.

Sorry to be so imprecise in my definition, but as I said, it is squishy! Your presence is your *je ne sais quoi*.

While the concept can be challenging to quantify or explain, we do know how to cultivate your presence. Focus attention on

- <u>Your awareness</u>: How you hold your conscious attention to the moment, what is going on with you, with others, and with the environment;

- <u>Your whole self</u>: An honest representation of your thoughts, emotions, memories, sensations in your body, values, concerns, intuitions, and whatever else you can bring to the moment;

- <u>Your intent</u>: What you plan to do, your reasons for doing it, how you plan to do it, and where you will intervene; and

- <u>Your curiosity</u>: Your attention to the people who are present and absent, patterns you observe, what may have shifted or changed over time, any hypotheses or learnings from the experience, and interest in whatever comes next.

Your presence may seem somewhat similar to your brand, in that it includes a set of perceptions and associations that people make when they regard you. But branding is more of a marketing exercise, an attempt to craft a distinctive image that helps "sell."

Presence is more than just a sales device. It is an integration of all of the elements of your persona (including the ones that might not appeal to a customer), for the purpose of supporting learning and change in others.

The clothes you wear, the language you use, whether you stand tall or stoop – all this and more are part of your presentation to the world. Whether you think about it or not, these artifacts send signals to the people around you, and evoke all sorts of reactions, presumptions, thoughts, and emotions. Every time you walk out the door you present a detailed message to the outside world about who you are and what you value.

Clothing is among the simplest artifacts to notice. Aspiring leaders are often advised to "dress for the job you want, not the job you have" (or in the old days, "Clothes make the man") because we tend to slot people in the professional hierarchy based on how they look. Fifty years ago, a man couldn't be taken seriously as a corporate leader unless he wore the appropriate suit and tie. Today, you may not be taken seriously as a corporate leader unless you sport the right hoodie, nose ring, and tattoo.

Of course, such signals can be used to deceive. Washington Post reporter Robin Ghivan pointed out that former US Rep. George Santos of New York was able to fabricate his entire life story and still get elected to Congress in 2022 because he looked the part he was trying to play. His preppy glasses, blazers, and sweaters conveyed to voters that he was a wealthy and successful businessman rather than the abject liar and fabulist he turned out to be.

Your presence is an integration of your past (your reputation, credentials, experience, etc.), your present (your values, how you show up, how you listen, how resilient you are, etc.), and your future (the kind of difference you'll make). Cultivating your presence makes you more interesting to others, which in turn increases your impact.

If this seems complex and confusing, don't worry: Nobody has it all figured out. There is no "right way" or "wrong way" to be, just an ongoing journey of reading, training, practice, and reflection in service of simply getting closer to your own personal ideal.

Some people are further along than others. They have "that certain something" we can't put our finger on. They don't speak the loudest or longest, dress the sharpest, or have the most impressive resume...but they wield enormous influence in almost any situation. They can "own the room" by being gregarious and outgoing, reserved, or even gruff. They convey quiet confidence and clarity, and bring others along. They use their presence to provide what's missing around them, and to model what's possible.

Some people can wow others with their charisma or charm, but the effects are fleeting. As author Dorothy Siminovich writes, "When we act authentically from our intentions, we create resonance with others, who then engage more openly and vibrantly with us." Long-standing connections come from that deeper place of presence.

Much like a comic book superpower, a powerful presence can be used for good or for evil. It can support, guide, empower, align, or illuminate...but it can also be used to manipulate, control, and maybe get you elected to Congress. (I credit The Daily Show host Leslie Jones with the best quote about Rep. Santos: "Do you know how much you have to lie to be known as 'the lying congressman??'")

No matter how firmly we establish our own presence, we can still be influenced by the presence of others. Consider mob psychology or herd mentality: When we become part of a large and emotional group, we can lose track of our personal boundaries and behave unexpectedly. In an angry mob, a peaceful person may become violent. In a rapturous group, a quiet person might begin to shout or dance. At a mournful moment, we might find ourselves crying, perhaps without even knowing why.

Enter a group of laughing friends, and you might involuntarily start laughing as well. It's as if we have suddenly become geese flying in perfect formation or fish swimming in a tightly packed school, each individual aligning our actions based on the signals we receive from others.

Even though we think of ourselves as wholly autonomous beings, we are extremely susceptible to "emotional contagion," moments when the presence and actions of others directly affect our own state of mind. There's nothing embarrassing here; our brains are simply built this way. This coming together feeds a deeply human need to create intimacy and connections with people who we see as similar to ourselves. We're constantly looking for our tribe and ways to align with it.

How does this happen? Scientists aren't sure. I've read a few theories, all of which sound pretty unsatisfying. Maybe we are sensing the electromagnetic signals from other people's vagus nerves (whatever those are). Or could it be our mirror neurons firing in unison? Does it matter?

# IMPACT

Regardless of the cause, we've all felt the vibe of a room and adapted to it, picking up on signals to make sure we resonate with those around us. In doing so, we are satisfying our own desires for intimacy and connection. We can cultivate our presence to be an instrument of change, but we must first understand ourselves before we can act effectively in support of others.

# Chapter 3

# Emotional Intelligence

Emotional intelligence (EI) is a critical tool for anyone hoping to increase their impact. People with high EI are able to monitor emotions in themselves and others, identify and label emotions appropriately, and then use that data effectively.

Yes, you can impress people by being smart, knowledgeable, or creative. But real impact comes from emotional intelligence, which enables you to build durable and productive relationships. At minimum, you need a certain amount of EI so your emotions don't get in your way, cloud your thinking, and distract you from the needs of others.

It is difficult work. Each of us must constantly guard against the pitfalls of self-delusion, egotism, and the power of the inner saboteur.

# IMPACT

Emotional data is continuously generated by our bodies, creating a rich and often overlooked source of feedback. This set of sensations and intuitions is ever-present, but many of us ignore or actively discount it, never learning to put names to the flood of feelings we experience every day.

Naming emotions seems rudimentary, yet for many people it's uncharted terrain. As famed engineer Nikola Tesla said more than a hundred years ago, "Most persons are so absorbed in the contemplation of the outside world that they are wholly oblivious to what is passing on within themselves."

In this century, a successful corporate manager in his 30s once admitted to me that he didn't know whether he experienced emotions at all. "Is 'confused' an emotion?" he asked. Another colleague recently grumped to me, "I don't fucking know how I feel!"

And they're not the only ones who are perplexed: Type "list of emotions" into a search engine and you'll find hundreds of suggestions for anyone at a loss for how to label their evanescent sensations.

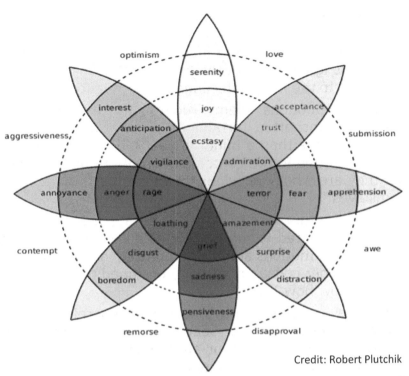

Credit: Robert Plutchik

Adding to the confusion, there is no simple and universally accepted taxonomy of emotions to help guide us. Aristotle had a list, and so did Darwin. American psychologist Paul Ekman identified six basic emotions: Happiness, sadness, fear, disgust, anger, and surprise. If that doesn't feel like enough complexity and detail, you can consult psychologist Robert Plutchik's rainbow-colored wheel based on eight fundamental emotional states.

There's value in getting it right. The Yale Center for Emotional Research asserts that "emotions drive learning, decision-making, creativity, relationships, and health." Their systematic approach starts with school-age children, teaching social and emotional learning focused on five skills to emotional intelligence: Recognizing, Understanding, Labeling, Expressing, and Regulating (RULER).

# IMPACT

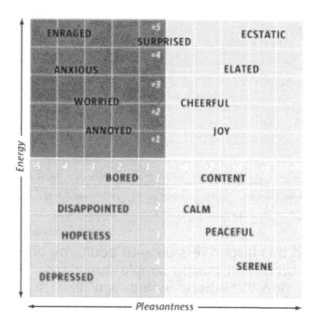

Credit: Yale Center for Emotional Research

To build familiarity with what's going on inside them, children are invited to point to a simple table with names of emotions appropriate to their age (plotted against high or low energy in the vertical axis, and more or less pleasant on the horizontal). After learning to identify and name their emotions, they are taught to develop appropriate behaviors to express what they're feeling, and to regulate emotions when they seem to get in the way.

It isn't just for kids. Yale's adult Mood Meter maps a hundred emotion words (and is also available as an app for iPhone or Android). The result is a more granular list that can help you name what you're feeling, explore different ways to express it, and devise a plan to shift (if you so choose) away from the red (high energy and high unpleasantness) to the yellow, blue, or green.

| | | | | | | | | | |
|---|---|---|---|---|---|---|---|---|---|
| Enraged | Panicked | Stressed | Jittery | Shocked | Surprised | Upbeat | Festive | Exhilarated | Ecstatic |
| Livid | Furious | Frustrated | Tense | Stunned | Hyper | Cheerful | Motivated | Inspired | Elated |
| Fuming | Frightened | Angry | Nervous | Restless | Energized | Lively | Enthusiastic | Optimistic | Excited |
| Anxious | Apprehensive | Worried | Irritated | Annoyed | Pleased | Happy | Focused | Proud | Thrilled |
| Repulsed | Troubled | Concerned | Uneasy | Peeved | Pleasant | Joyful | Hopeful | Playful | Blissful |
| Disgusted | Glum | Disappointed | Down | Apathetic | At Ease | Easygoing | Content | Loving | Fulfilled |
| Pessimistic | Morose | Discouraged | Sad | Bored | Calm | Secure | Satisfied | Grateful | Touched |
| Alienated | Miserable | Lonely | Disheartened | Tired | Relaxed | Chilled | Restful | Blessed | Balanced |
| Despondent | Depressed | Sullen | Exhausted | Fatigued | Mellow | Thoughtful | Peaceful | Comfy | Carefree |
| Despairing | Hopeless | Desolate | Spent | Drained | Sleepy | Complacent | Tranquil | Cozy | Serene |

High Energy ↑ / Low Energy ↓

Unpleasant ← → Pleasant

Credit: Yale Center for Emotional Research

I've used this larger version with adults by offering them a printed table and posing simple questions: "Where are you right now?" "Where would you like to be?" And: "What's one thing you might do to shift to a better spot?" Even when a person can't settle on a word that captures the essence of their emotional state, they can still point to a region of the table that seems to describe where they are, and another where they'd like to land. Once they've raised their awareness of the emotional terrain, it's possible to conceptualize how they might make that jump.

I know from personal experience that just being able to recognize, acknowledge, and label an emotion helps give me some agency over it. Once I have a name for what's going on inside, I can alter my "state of mind" (the meaning I make), and how I act as a result.

To whit: The anger I feel when I'm cut-off by another car while driving is unavoidable; what I make of that anger is up to me. I might choose to dwell on the injustice of what happened, or the foolishness of the other driver. I might use the experience to reinforce an unflattering generalization in my mind about "people like that." The states of mind that follow my emotion – resentment, blaming, stereotyping – might feel energizing to me, even if they are counterproductive or irrational.

Or I could choose another path. I could notice and acknowledge my anger, and then minimize its power by focusing on the fact that nobody was hurt in the incident. I could look ahead to arriving safely at my destination, reorienting my state of mind towards gratitude, relief, and anticipation.

I've used this very redirection on many occasions to manage strong and unpleasant emotions that used to overwhelm me. I've come to learn that any anger, resentment, or anxiety I might feel can be completely drained of its energy when I am able to focus instead on my gratitude.

A while back I confronted a puzzling situation in my professional life that required some similar emotional jiu-jitsu: Although I have led large and small groups for almost thirty years, at some point I started experiencing queasy feelings before beginning a session. I was confident in myself and my work, but I still felt flush, my mouth got dry, and I started to perspire.

For a while, I suppressed my awareness of what was happening. Over time I started to notice the pattern. I began to name the emotions I was feeling (anxiety, fear, self-doubt), which allowed me to experience them and make meaning of my situation.

I didn't like this new sweaty, anxious pattern; my emotions were getting in the way of me doing my job. So I renamed my feelings as "excitement and anticipation," which almost immediately lessened their sting.

Now when I feel the tingling and perspiration start to build, I welcome it. I'm not nervous, I tell myself. I'm just excited! This reframing enables me use the burst of pre-meeting energy to my advantage, rather than having it hold me back.

I'm not the only one thinking about EI. "Emotional intelligence" has become part of the corporate lexicon of catch phrases and ideas-of-the-moment. To break into the mainstream, EI advocates had to replace the old archetype of the work environment as all business, where sentiment, intuition, or emotions were scorned as inappropriate. Professionals were to only concern themselves with cold, hard facts. Feelings and other soggy concepts were irrelevant in the world of cold-eyed decision-making.

That outdated caricature crumbled because it's patriarchal hogwash that doesn't work very well. As I noted in Chapter 2, leaders can't just issue orders and expect meek employees to fall into line. They need to build relationships to cultivate their influence, balancing the care people crave against other workplace goals. Leaders must demonstrate respect for others' emotions, even when they are inconvenient.

Studies demonstrate the connection between Emotional Intelligence and the bottom line. Google's Aristotle Project found that the most successful teams had "high average social sensitivity," meaning that team members quickly perceived their colleagues' feelings by noticing verbal and non-verbal clues. The least effective teams showed the opposite pattern.

Cultivating your own Emotional Intelligence is more important than ever because the need for empathetic and effective leaders is so great, and so many of us still have difficulty making sense of our emotional terrain. Now is the time to start tuning your antenna to the emotions that exist, so you can have real impact raising awareness and liberating others' energy.

For example, the next time you're in a group you might take a step back and observe how interpersonal dynamics might affect your mood. What feelings come up for you when there is conflict? How does it feel when a decision gets made? Make note of your emotions when people in the group connect with one another. Notice what happens for you when someone demonstrates their individuality, or sets themselves at the center or margins of a conversation.

Noticing and naming your own emotions can be a transformative intervention that becomes a habit, and eventually builds a sharper EI. But while looking inward is a key first step, it's not a magic wand. For example, you can never be certain which emotions any other person is experiencing, even when they tell you. And as the Yale research suggests, sometimes you can't even know for sure what emotions you're experiencing.

Someone may cry during a conversation: Is that sadness? Fatigue? Relief? Melancholy? Anger? Frustration? Does the behavior connect with something that was just said, a relationship with someone in the room, or to a person who isn't even present? Are they responding to a memory, something in the moment, or an anticipated future? Are they having an emotional reaction, or a physical reaction? Maybe it's allergies...?

Regardless of the role you play in a given conversation, the best course might be to collect data, hold your curiosity, and be ready to raise awareness of the here and now. You might name what you've observed, or simply watch with eyes open, mouth shut, and empathy available...which can be an impactful intervention all by itself.

When I see curious data, I always have the choice to either remark on it or hold back. Sometimes I'll find myself bubbling inside, eager to find a gap in the discussion to insert my insight or do something that will call attention to what I'm observing. In some cases, I'll give in to that energy and voice an observation. In other cases, I'll hold my tongue and count to thirty...just to see what happens next. Maybe someone else will remark on what I've seen, or the group may ignore the data, or the situation might change radically or deepen. Holding back as a facilitator (rather than jumping in) often reaps its own rewards.

If I see behaviors that spark my curiosity, I'll be more likely to jump in. Raw expressions of emotion are very rare in work settings, but when they occur they dominate everyone's attention. These are crucial moments for any leader, and it's crucial to balance the need for honesty and openness against concern for the well-being of every person in the conversation.

I'm particularly careful about how and when I might call attention to a person's expression of emotion when others are around. I don't want to put anyone needlessly in the spotlight.

# IMPACT

When I do intervene, I'll choose my words judiciously to demonstrate I'm not presuming I know what's going on. I might say, "It appears like you're having a reaction there," or "I notice you're wiping your eyes," and then see what happens. (Note that my comments are about the data I can observe, rather than any assumptions I might draw.) If the person wants to address their experience, he or she can say so. If they'd rather keep it to themselves, they can do that too. Their response will inform whatever I do next.

Many times, I'll be guided by my intuition: I'll just have a sense that some emotion is in the air. Or I might feel one of several physical manifestations in my body that I recognize as my own patterns of response. When I experience tension, my right shoulder tightens, or I sense a fluttering in my stomach. When I'm anxious, I often perspire or feel tingling in my hands. And when I'm overwhelmed, I can get a powerful desire to flee...or I become extremely fatigued.

Recognizing these clues in myself sparks my curiosity. I'll interrogate what I'm feeling and try to name my emotions, and then wonder what may be prompting them. And once I recognize my own emotional state, I'll become curious about others around me. (Experience has shown that if I'm feeling something strongly, it's likely that someone else may be feeling something similar.) The task of noticing data that align or diverge from my impressions helps me choose how to intervene.

For anyone hoping to have greater impact, awareness and insight about emotions represents a kind of gold mine. There's always tons of data to explore! On a given day with one of my clients, this process can repeat itself over and over and with different levels of intensity. I might notice data and name an emotion, wonder about its significance, and decide what to do...and then start another cycle of observation moments later. In later chapters, I'll dig more deeply into how you can mine that data to provide transformational support to others.

Even when we try, it's practically impossible to eliminate emotions from our perceptions and decision-making.

# IMPACT

Unless you're a robot (and if you are, why are you reading this book?) your emotions will color and inform every action you take. Becoming more emotionally literate is therefore essential to developing influence, so you can be as effective and impactful as possible in whatever circumstance you find yourself.

# Chapter 4

# Listening

One characteristic that distinguishes the best leaders from their less-effective brethren is the ability to listen. This is especially true in my profession. Good consultants listen; bad consultants are too busy doing something else.

Of course, we're all distracted to some degree. We live in a distracted world. Most of us think we're listening to those around us when we're often just thinking about ourselves. We might be dazzled by what happened before, or pre-occupied about what we have to do next. Or we may be strip-mining the conversation at hand to find an idea that allows us to refocus attention on what we want to talk about, or the story we want to tell. Or maybe we're just looking at a screen and barely listening at all.

Not listening is epidemic. We glance at our watches or check our phones during even the most intimate conversations. When I meet with people in their offices, they often peek at their computers, click their keyboards, or shuffle papers during our conversation. In meetings, this is called "social loafing" – participants are present in body but are content to let others in the group pay attention and do all the work.

Many of us start not listening from the very moment we meet someone new. People often tell me, "I can't remember names," which makes me wonder what they are doing when they're not listening to the person in front of them say their name.

For many like me, the challenge of listening is the challenge of patience. I am often too quick to respond when I hear something compelling. I have to fight the urge to respond instantly to the first shiny object I perceive. And I can mesmerize myself with the wise and pithy thing I want to say next.

The little devil and the little angel are both perched on my shoulders at that moment. The devil is screaming, "Show this person how smart and funny you are!" "Slow down," the angel is reassuring. "Listen to what is being said."

On the other end of the spectrum, I don't want to disparage zoning-out; it's a valuable skill when used with discretion. It's OK to not listen intently every minute of every day. We all use our lower levels of listening to filter out meaningless drivel and tiresome people, and to conserve our energy for the moments and relationships that really matter.

Effective leaders like those I described in Chapter 1 minimize distraction and cultivate their listening skills. This allows them to collect more data about what's going on, what's important and what's not, and how they can help others attain their goals. They get in touch with the current moment by paying attention to it.

Some call this mindfulness. Professor Jon Kabat-Zinn of the University of Massachusetts Medical School defines it as "paying attention in a particular way, on purpose, in the present moment, and nonjudgmentally."

When I'm facilitating, I'll typically follow the flow of the conversation to stay engaged and model good listening habits for others. But at the same time, I'm intentionally *not listening*, so I can pay attention to the big picture of where we are in our work, and where we have to go. My ability to simultaneously listen and not listen enables me to see both the forest and the trees in support of the group's goals.

At other times, I'll play-up my ignorance to check what I'm hearing. I'll use phrases like, *"Help me understand..."* or *"Can you say more about...?"* I've found numerous instances in which a commonly-used word or phrase has meant different things to different people. The technique has enabled me to tease-out unexamined assumptions and pat thinking that had been there all along but which nobody had ever noticed.

Meaning often goes far beyond the surface of the words we use. Throughout my work, I try to listen with empathy for the deeper emotional and intellectual import of a moment. Focusing too much on the most obvious data can distract from what's really going on in a conversation.

In such cases I heed the advice of poet Alice Duer Miller to take a "vigorous, human interest in what is being told us." Or I think of my mother's plea: "Don't listen to what I said. Listen to what I mean!"

Many of us know the term Active Listening, in which the listener gestates on what is being said and reflects back to the speaker elements of his or her statements. Being in Active Listening mode allows me to organize in my mind what's being said, and then demonstrate to the speaker that I've heard it. Staying quiet, mirroring the ideas and feelings expressed, and communicating this clearly back to the speaker helps me establish a deeper connection, and models respect.

Former US Senator and author S.I. Hayakawa framed it this way in his 1962 book *The Use and Misuse of Language*:

"Listening means trying to see the problem the way the speaker sees it – which means not sympathy...but empathy, which is experiencing (the moment) with him. Listening requires entering actively and imaginatively into the other fellow's situation and trying to understand a frame of reference different from your own." (And yes: I notice that Hayakawa only seems interested in listening to "fellows." You may draw your own conclusions.)

In addition to the "one foot in, one foot out" dynamic, a leader also zooms in close to the specific words and content, but then helicopters-up to see the bigger picture of what is being accomplished, who's engaged and who's not, and how the conversation fits into larger goals.

As I noted earlier, I periodically stop listening with intent...but in some cases, my checking-out is just self-defense because the topic being discussed is too complicated or arcane for me to understand. For instance, while working recently with a group of geneticists, biologists, and data scientists, their conversation turned to various approaches for studying neurodevelopmental diseases related to complex copy-number variants and other chromosomal anomalies.

I could loosely follow some of the discussion, but my 1980s-era undergraduate degree in Government and Spanish didn't prepare me for all of that 21st century science and confusing vocabulary. (Remind me again what "etiology" and "phenotype" mean?) Too much of what they discussed was well-beyond my generalist base of knowledge. Trying to stay abreast of every idea would have forced me to repeatedly interrupt their flow and ask for explanations about things that they all understood.

And trying to catch up to their level would have hurt my brain.

So I pulled back and stopped attempting to grasp every nuance. I paid attention to the energy in the group, who was speaking and who was silent, and any emotional cues I could perceive. I wondered to myself: Does this conversation still seem productive? In what ways are people responding to what's being said? Are people speaking quickly and loudly, or slowly and softly?

When it seemed like the energy had started to wane, I invited someone to summarize where the discussion had ended up. (I surely couldn't have done it!) When a participant framed what had been said, it solidified the conversational thread and enabled us to move on to the next topic. It was another case in which my *not listening* had served the interests of the group. Pulling back allowed me to see the conversation more fully, and it gave participants the opportunity to demonstrate leadership by articulating their collective take-aways.

On the other hand, some conversations are too tempting for me to leave alone. Even though I may be present as an outsider, I sometimes want to jump into the middle and get deeply involved in a juicy discussion that's happening in front of me. When I notice myself being seduced by the content, I'll make a concerted effort to push my attention back out to the periphery and reinforce my "one-foot-in, one-foot-out" stance.

In those moments I'll use two simple physical gestures to bolster my self-discipline. First, I'll discretely take a half step backwards; then I'll hold my hands palm-up in front of me. These invisible interventions break my focus on the ebb and flow of what's being discussed, and help me take in the totality of the group. The gestures remind me to shift my attention from the trees to the forest, and to listen less closely so I can notice other data in the environment.

At other times, I'll find myself lulled into indifference by a conversation. Instead of wanting to jump into the middle, I want to leave the room. Maybe it's because I've lost the thread of what's being discussed; maybe it's because the topic just doesn't interest me.

When this happens, I'll first stop and ask myself why. What's making me want to pull away rather than stay engaged? Is it just me, or are others checking-out too?

As I'll discuss in later chapters, there are many forms of resistance that can sap the energy of a meeting and make it difficult to pay attention; I'll share more specific interventions for how to address these barriers later on.

In such situations, I'll first take basic steps to revive my physical energy. If sitting, I'll stand or move to another location. I'll get something to drink or snag that last brownie from the dessert tray. And just like any other person in the room, I'll always have the option of calling attention to what I'm experiencing just to see if it breaks the dynamic.

A basic observation could do the trick. I might say, "I notice I'm having difficulty following the conversation now," and then see what happens.

Listening (and not listening) are both skills, which means they can be honed through intention and practice. There is nothing magical about being a good listener; it's just someone who is paying attention to what matters.

Listening fosters connection and intimacy, which is useful in almost any environment. And by modeling good listening, we help others adapt and hone their behaviors as well.

The result is a deeper conversation about more meaningful topics. Listening well enables the Gestalt practitioner to hold a space for both transactionalism and contact in support of the group's larger goals.

# Chapter 5

# Figure and Ground, and Multiple Realities

When you start listening carefully, you'll notice that there's a lot of static mixed in with the signal. It can be difficult to make sense of conflicting information, and it gets messy trying to sort it all – discerning anecdotal and empirical data from perceptions, opinions, beliefs, and attitudes.

It's not uncommon for people in an important discussion to realize at some point that things have become an unmanageable jumble. Participants recognize that they're not understanding one another, and that the topics don't seem to fit together. Some people may be focusing on causes, and others on effects. Some may be energized by opportunities while others are held back by perceived risks.

Some may be fixated on the past, while others are trying to look into the future.

At this point, it can get really ugly really fast. Emotions can quickly escalate. Colleagues may call one another out for irritating habits or patterns of behavior. People who feel they are typically ignored might complain that they are not being heard (yet again). Someone may complain loudly that the entire process is a waste of time. People may start to suspect they are on a sinking ship.

It's not: It's just the muddle in the middle, the uncomfortable and unpleasant place author Sam Kaner calls "the Groan Zone." It's the moment at which well-meaning people start to diverge, sometimes about everything. People may have different views about what matters, or what should be done. They may not even agree on what they're talking about.

A feeling of hopelessness is common in the Groan Zone, and it can lead some people to react harshly. They may question the process, try to escape, lash out at colleagues, or rush through to the safety of a convenient solution. That's because humans are naturally problem-solvers, and our entire lives of school and work have rewarded us for "figuring it out." We're programmed to move from disorder to resolution, and it's deeply irritating when our progress feels blocked.

Sadly, "figuring it out" is getting harder than ever. Today's world is so volatile, uncertain, complex, and ambiguous that we now have a handy acronym – VUCA – to describe our predicament. **V**olatility: Things are changing faster than ever before, and the rate of change is increasing geometrically. **U**ncertainty: Surprise is the new normal, as shocking "black swan" events (e.g., pandemics, droughts, tsunamis, earthquakes, market crashes, etc.) are everywhere. **C**omplexity: Our institutions and systems are so big and multi-faceted that nobody, not even their creators, can reliably predict how they will function, how they can be subverted, where they will break down, or how they can be fixed. **A**mbiguity: We all face a continual "haze of war," with a deluge of information and little clarity about how to discern the truth.

Sorry: We can't do anything about the existence of VUCA or the Groan Zone. And that's not all bad. There can be benefit to the chaos and jumble if managed effectively. The keys are to accept their presence and find ways to adapt to their effects.

This is a moment when the Gestalt intervener can provide real value, first by normalizing the feelings of despair and disarray these dynamics may provoke. Participants will want to speed ahead to blow through the discomfort, so it's essential for Gestaltist leaders to project calm and slow things down. In doing so, two valuable models can support your efforts to find a way out of the confusion.

## Figure and ground

Every scene has a figure and ground. Imagine a photo in which one object, a vase with flowers, is in focus while the rest of the photo (the table holding the flowers, and the person sitting beside it) are out of focus. In this case, the photographer has called our attention to the vase and flowers, making them the figure, and pushing the other objects out of focus, making them the ground. When we look at this photo, we see the table and person as context for the beauty of the flowers and vase.

A second photo of the exact same scene might put the person in focus (making it the figure), while blurring the vase and flowers, making them part of the ground. And a third photo might focus on the bud on one flower, making it the figure and everything else the ground. The three photos all contain the exact same data, but our sense of what we're looking at is radically different. The first is a picture of a floral arrangement. The second is a picture of a person. The third is an examination of a specific flower.

The figure holds our attention. The ground provides its context.

# IMPACT

The figure/ground model acknowledges that while we may observe multiple objects in a situation, we can only really focus on one aspect at a time...and when our attention shifts to a different figure, our perception of the entire scene changes. In a simple photo, the figure is often easy to distinguish when we perceive the visual clues of color, focus, light, and shadow. But when observing a complex human and social construct (like the issues confronting a leadership team that's just merged with another organization), the clarity of figure and ground can be difficult to discern.

In a recent class I attended, the instructor shared a simple demonstration of how this concept can apply in daily life. As she stood in front of the group, she read from a set of index cards she had prepared, each of which contained a simple description of her. As she read each card, she placed it face-up on the floor in front of her:

"Woman."

"White."

"Sister."

"Extravert."

"Boss."

"Jazz lover."

"Lesbian."

"Car owner."

"Mother."

"Teacher."

"College graduate."

Each descriptor she read was an element of her identity. In that moment, as she stood in front of us, this set of characteristics formed her ground. Which elements were figural? The answer could be different for each observer, and it could change from moment to moment.

For me, her voice was figural: I noticed it was warm and firm, and it drew me in. I also made note of her confident posture, and the fact that she was speaking with a slight Philadelphia accent. And I enjoyed the demonstration of figure and ground that she was sharing (which is why I'm recounting it here), so I made a note to myself so I could remember it. For me in that moment, the method was figural.

For one of my classmates, something else might have been figural. It might be her role as a mother, and how that guided her relationship with us as her students. Or it could be a question about how her identification as a white person might affect her relationships with people of similar or different ethnic and racial backgrounds.

In that circumstance, all those interpretations could be valid. And five seconds later, someone might make a comment that shifts all of our perceptions. Suddenly a different set of insights into what is figure and ground might emerge, and the original insights might recede. The task for the Gestaltist isn't to come up with a single, satisfying, permanent, and ontologically correct answer for what is figure and ground. Our work is to make note of what might be there, and to notice what is catching and holding our attention in any given moment.

When interacting with a client, I try to seek and collect data without locking any figure firmly into my mind. The figure is tentative because I don't really know what will ultimately matter for the work I am about to do. In my first interaction I might notice the way she holds her identity as a boss. Later I notice that she has always worked in large organizations with rigid hierarchies, and that she drives a Tesla. Will any of these data points matter to our work or our relationship? It's impossible to know.

Especially at the start, I must have the discipline to hold those figures very lightly. I think of this as "sketching the figure in pencil," an acknowledgement that my initial impressions of figure and ground are tentative, speculative, and likely to be erased and scribbled over many times. This mental picture helps me resist the urge to fixate quickly on one figure while prematurely dismissing everything else.

In every situation, it takes time and flexibility before you can land on figures that feel both durable and useful.

Developing such helpful figures is a key element of the Gestalt practice.

## Multiple Realities

We've all had the experience of listening to someone describe a situation that we ourselves also witnessed and feeling confounded by how strange their version of the story sounds. How is it we could have seen the exact same things and come away with a completely different understanding of what happened?

Japanese filmmaker Akira Kurosawa explored this phenomenon in his acclaimed 1950 movie *Rashomon*, in which four witnesses give contradictory accounts of a single murder they each observed. The "Rashomon effect" is now recognized as a storytelling technique that emphasizes the unreliability of any one perspective over any other.

In the Indian parable of the Blind Men and the Elephant (which may date to 500 BCE) a group of blind men come across an elephant for the first time. The first approaches the trunk and declares, "The elephant is much like a snake!" Another man touches the tusk and says, "No, the elephant is like a spear." A third man touches the elephant's tail: "Incorrect! The elephant is much like a rope!" The fourth man touches the elephant's side, and says, "You are all wrong. The elephant is very much like a wall." Of course, each blind man in the parable is correct in their own way. To some degree, an elephant is a bit like a snake, a spear, a rope, and a wall, while in sum it is not really like any of those things.

Every day, each of us forms our perceptions of the world based on what we've experienced in the past, and what we need to survive and thrive in the present. If we've only ever touched a tusk, our reality must be that an elephant is much like a spear...and we'll never accept that it's really like a wall. (Or a rope.)

As Gestalt practitioners, much of our work is to surface the multiple realities that exist within a group or organization, acknowledging each as valid and deserving of respect. And once those conflicting, overlapping, and confusing realities are seen and accepted, participants can work together towards a shared figure that everyone can accept.

This concept often shows up for me when a client hires me to "get everyone on board" with an organizational plan, or "buy in" to a new strategy that the senior leaders have created. Often, these plans and strategies have been created by people who now want my help to convince everyone else that their perception of "the elephant" is the correct one.

Of course, the leader's perceptions are valid...but so are everyone else's. At the top, the leader typically has a view of the broader organizational environment, but less sense of what it's like "in the trenches." Similarly, junior employees may know the ins and outs of their department, while having little sense of the bigger picture. Both realities have value, but it's usually the senior leaders who try to force their realities on those below them, and rarely the other way around. In such cases, a big part of my role is to hold a space for the input of less powerful stakeholders, helping them voice their realities early in the process before all the important decisions are made.

It's the Gestaltist's role to recognize that there are multiple realities, and to raise awareness of the importance of those perceptions. And it's the leader's role to decide how far to go in reconciling those different realities before moving forward.

Few processes can be held open until everyone in the organization comes around to a single and unambiguous view of the way things are; eventually, processes must come to an end and decisions must be made. As I like to remind my clients, their organizations are not democracies, so they shouldn't feel frozen if, after a reasonable effort to get alignment, some people persist in seeing things differently. (And even democratic processes rarely end in unanimous votes.)

# IMPACT

What matters for any leader is that everyone feels in the end that their reality was acknowledged and respected. It's our job to hold a space for these conflicting perspectives to be aired and explored, honor them as valid, and help bring a group to accept what is.

Sometimes the resulting answer is messy and unsatisfying, but it may be the best the group can do. Despite their wishes for a neat and pat reconciliation, the group may have to accept difference, uncertainty, and a multitude of irreconcilable realities that are present within the organization.

# IMPACT

# Part 2: The Middle

*"A story should have
a beginning, a middle, and an end...
but not necessarily in that order."*

Jean-Luc Godard

# Chapter 6
# Making Meaning

When my clients call me, it's often because something has gone wrong. Maybe their last meeting was a fiasco, or they're tired of all the procrastination and indecision. Maybe trust is down and bickering is up. At other times, clients call because a big need is looming – something like, "We have to increase revenue!" or "We want to finally be proactive, instead of just running around like crazy people with our hair on fire."

Before they make the call to me, those proto-clients have to first make meaning of what's going on in their world. Their act of "making meaning" is the critical step of assembling data into a story or a picture ("a figure") that describes a situation...and hopefully sets my lucrative consulting project into motion.

I'm always grateful when the client presents me with a clear figure in that first call. I'm grateful, but deeply skeptical. Don't take it personal, clients: I'm skeptical because I know that we humans have such a mediocre record of making meaning in complex situations filled with fallible, unreliable humans and all of their confusing, contradictory data.

Whenever we try to make meaning, we tend to rush. We tend to ignore our blind spots. We protect our egos. We zoom in when we should zoom out, and zoom out when we should zoom in. We get a lot wrong, and what's worse is that we don't even know it.

All of which is problematic because once any of us settles on a figure, that picture tends to get mentally locked-in. And once a figure is locked-in, we start ignoring any data that might challenge that meaning.

We THINK we see the world with total clarity even though our senses deceive us every day, providing imperfect and incomplete conclusions about what's around us. Looking at a digital photo in 2015, a portion of the world saw a blue and black dress, while the rest saw a white and gold dress. If you saw a blue and black dress, you probably couldn't fathom how anyone could see something else...and vice-versa. Similarly, many of us were dumbfounded in 2018 by a digital recording: How could some of us hear the word "laurel," and others just as clearly hear "yanny"? Which cohort of people was right? Both? Neither?

Once we have what we believe to be the facts, it's human nature to jump to conclusions about what those facts mean. While today's world puts a premium on acting fast, in a time of VUCA (when so much of the data we receive is volatile, uncertain, complex, and ambiguous) making meaning too soon can be a far bigger risk. When we settle too quickly on an erroneous or incomplete figure, we are more likely to choose an intervention that's badly adapted to what's really going on. The bottom line is: Don't believe everything you think.

Gestalt interveners work to slow the impulse to make meaning quickly. We hold our conclusions lightly, and encourage clients to do the same. This is difficult, because many of us fly from collecting data to taking action without considering any of the subtle and discrete steps that exist in between.

This is when the Ladder of Inference, a concept developed by Harvard Business School Professor Chris Argyris, becomes useful. At the base of the Ladder of Inference are all the sights, sounds, smells, tastes, textures, ideas, and emotions that swirl around us every minute of every day. In a way, each of us is like a fish swimming in a vast sea of such data. Just as the fish is oblivious to the water, you and I are oblivious to almost all the data that surrounds us throughout our lives.

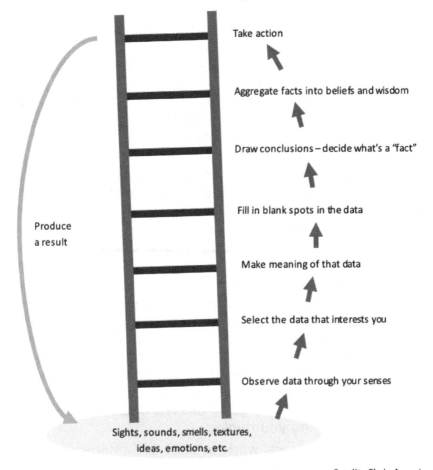

Take action

Aggregate facts into beliefs and wisdom

Draw conclusions – decide what's a "fact"

Fill in blank spots in the data

Produce a result

Make meaning of that data

Select the data that interests you

Observe data through your senses

Sights, sounds, smells, textures, ideas, emotions, etc.

Credit: Chris Argyris

# IMPACT

You take in most of that data through your senses – sounds you can hear, wavelengths of light you can see, smells you can detect, emotions you can feel, and intuitions you can articulate. From all the input that's available, you select only the most interesting stimuli to notice, and filter everything else out of your awareness. Without realizing it, each of us is constantly ignoring data that appears useless or inconsequential, sensations like the feel of your shoe pressing on your foot, or the sound of a car passing a block away.

When interesting data gets through your filters, you start to make meaning of what you've observed by applying the lessons of your past experiences and the values of your culture. For example, you might wake up one morning to the sound of a siren and recognize immediately that something important is happening.

Since we almost never have all the data we need, humans have become extremely adept at filling in the blanks and sorting through noise to make educated guesses and assumptions. In fact, we are master blank fillers and noise sorters. When you or I see a familiar letter or number missing a detail, we make the leap and identify the figure as if it were whole; this is why Captcha systems on the Internet are effective at distinguishing between people and computers. If this clump of lines and colors looks to you like the letters "D" "O" and "E," you may click on the box to assert you are human.

Let's go back to that siren you heard. It didn't pass by; in fact, the truck with the siren stopped out front. Maybe the emergency is in your house?

# IMPACT

As the fog of confusion clears, you assemble enough relevant data to draw conclusions. This is the deeply satisfying (but potentially disturbing) moment when uncertainty diminishes and your hypotheses harden into "facts." With the sound of firefighters stomping up your stairs and the faint whiff of smoke, you conclude that something is burning nearby, and a crisis is at hand.

Over the course of your life, you've strung together similar facts and experiences over and over, assimilating them into your own personal wisdom and set of beliefs, all of which inform your choices. Perhaps you've put out a small fire before, so rushing to help might seem like an option. Or you might remember your childhood safety training and conclude that the only prudent course of action is to pull on your pants and get out of the house.

The actions you might take (or don't take) at the top of the Ladder of Inference – which is very different from the ladder the fire department just leaned against your house – are the direct result of ascending each of the previous steps. Whatever you do, or fail to do, produces a result, which in turn creates new data that you can observe through your senses. Thus, the process of climbing the Ladder of Inference begins all over again.

It is useful to remember that much of what each of us thinks of as "fact" doesn't necessarily derive from some irrefutable trove of cosmic truth, but is often the product of our vantage point in the moment mixed with our emotions and life experiences. As I discussed in the previous discussion of multiple realities, no two people sense the world in the same way, and each of us filters the available data through our own unique sieve. Once people start sifting, selecting, imbuing with meaning, and filling-in the blanks based on their cultural perspectives and personal habits, every conclusion starts to look a little less solid.

My background in politics and Gestalt have taught me to approach facts with a degree of skepticism. In my world, data rarely leads to clear-cut indisputable facts. Mostly it leads to hypotheses – tentative explanations or meanings that can be joined by multiple alternate hypotheses, or completely supplanted by another more persuasive hypothesis at any time.

OK, sure: There are empirical facts: The Earth rotates on its axis, which means the sun rises in the east. But what these facts mean, and what significance they hold is subject to widely varying interpretations by different people at different times. If you're lost in the woods, knowing where the sun rises can be critical. For an artist or writer, this fact may be nothing more than a hackneyed metaphor.

Making meaning is essential, but it must be done carefully and with intention.

- Take your time (but not too much). I often advise clients to "sit with their ambiguity" and collect more data before settling on a figure. But don't sit in confusion forever, because no matter how long you wait you will probably never have enough data. At some point, an imperfect figure may be better than nothing.

- Gather data widely. Engaging more voices and perspectives produces more credible and solid facts. The missing clue to resolve a puzzling figure is often waiting in plain sight, and you might need to bring in someone with a completely different set of views and biases to see the obvious truths right in front of you. In big organizations, it's often the frontline people (e.g., nurses, call-center operators, janitors, etc.) who hold critical data that the leaders ignore but desperately need.

- Hold your meaning lightly. Accept that you'll never have all the insight you need, so let go of the conceit that your figure will ever be 100% correct, valid, or durable. Even "sure things" will have to be re-examined when the circumstances change or new evidence emerges.

As the African proverb says, "If you want to go fast, go alone. If you want to far, go together" – and it's only possible to go far if you open yourself up to others and their perspectives. More data from more sources yields a richer figure, and more confidence in the meaning you can derive.

Making meaning is a critical and distinct step in the Gestalt process. And even though the meaning we make is almost always tentative and uncertain, leaders of all kinds must remain optimistic that even flawed meanings can support our work and the people around us.

# Chapter 7

# Intervening with Intention

As a consultant, I get hired only when three vital criteria are met, a situation consultant David Fields calls the Client Trust Triangle. I have to show my client that I have their needs in mind, that I won't screw things up by wasting their time or money (or worse: betraying their secrets), and that I'll be of help.

Most clients will give me some time and space to collect data and make meaning...but ultimately, they're paying me to intervene and have impact. That said, I can't simply show up and "do something." I have to get the lay of the land, and then add some distinctive element, a perspective or approach that doesn't already exist within their system.

The same is true when your boss assigns you to a new project. Or when a colleague takes the time and energy to bring you in to an ongoing conversation. They're looking for something new, different, and impactful. They're looking for help.

It pays to know what kind of help they have in mind. Usually, people are looking for First Order Change, outcomes that are incremental and continuous, and may involve modest updates to systems, processes, or structures. First Order Changes leave existing core values and identity intact; they are tweaks around the edges that support continuity and order.

To achieve First Order Change, the team must find ways to "do it better." In such cases, my role as a consultant is to support ideas and improvements from within the current context. We'll try to rock the boat a little bit without making it capsize.

Second Order Changes, in contrast, are deeply disruptive. These are the kinds of transformational and revolutionary actions valorized by Facebook founder Mark Zuckerberg's quest to "move fast and break things." Second Order Changes alter an organization (or a sector) at its core.

To achieve Second Order Changes, stakeholders strive to "make it different." My role in such cases is to support a trusting environment that allows participants to think outside of the box, challenge assumptions, and embrace outlandish ideas. We'll devote time to finding inspiration and fueling imagination. We'll open the space for conflict and confusion, and combat the tendency to think small and avoid risk. We'll flip the metaphorical boat over if we have to.

Regardless of the degree of change my client seeks, I strive to be of service and intervene with intention. And to guide my work, I hold in my mind a useful Gestalt concept, The Four Roles of the Intervener:

- Sensing: As I noted previously, everything I may experience as a practitioner has the potential to be germane to the client and the project. I continually take note of the "here and now," paying attention to anything that I may see, feel, hear, smell, taste, or sense intuitively that might be useful to the group.

- Observing: After the sensation is recognized, I look for patterns and connections to other data that may have emerged. If no patterns are apparent, perhaps the data can be set aside. But if, for example, I notice goosebumps on my arm and the person next to me is putting on their sweater, I might infer that those two data points may be connected.

- Conceptualizing: This is the point when I make meaning of the data and decide what's relevant. The meaning may be in the form of a hypothesis (e.g., "I wonder if someone left the window open.") or a metaphor (e.g., "It feels like we're in the deep freeze.")

- Intervening: After noticing and recognizing data, looking for patterns, and developing a hypothesis about what's going on, it's time to intervene in support of the group. Paradoxically, one possible intervention is to do nothing. (I'll say more about that later.)

Like me, you might habitually rush through all four of these steps and go blindly to intervention without taking the time to consider the other three roles. There is power though in taking these steps more slowly.

Lingering in sensation provides insight into how it may feel for others in the room. And it opens me up to data that could be essential in fully mobilizing the group's energy for change. In fact, this "here and now" data is typically ignored by clients who set their attention elsewhere – often on the future or the past, or on people and forces that are not present in the moment.

As I'll explain in the chapter about the Paradoxical Theory of Change, I know that lasting change is likely to be achieved only after the "here and now" is fully acknowledged and accepted. Staying longer in sensation is a powerful tool to help that happen.

For most of my career, I skipped directly through sensing and observing in the blink of an eye and went instantly to conceptualization. In doing so, I blithely discarded any sensations or observations that didn't fit with my instantly developed hypotheses.

When I found my eyelids getting heavy during a meeting, I didn't sit with the heaviness in my eyes and consider what it might mean: Instead, I just forced myself to get another cup of coffee. When I felt a tingling in my belly, I wrote it off as nervousness without noticing what happened moments before that might have prompted that sensation.

Now, I try to stay longer in the "here and now," to experience the perceptions I feel in my body and wonder what patterns might exist. Then I consider what meaning those patterns might hold.

Once I've settled on a hypothesis, the time arrives to intervene, to consider adding something to the process that will interrupt the flow and support a change that will serve the group's needs. I may choose to:

- Heighten awareness, giving voice to some observable data such as, "I notice several people are talking at once." This allows others in the group to see what's happening too, and lets them decide how and whether to respond. Many people aren't used to hearing this kind of intervention, so it may have the effect of stopping a conversation cold. In other cases, a well-timed observation can empower someone else to comment on a troublesome pattern (e.g., "We're always talking all over each other!" or "Nobody ever listens to me!"), or the group may begin to police themselves.

- Offer a hypothesis: I may choose to make meaning of the data that's been observed and share that tentative figure with the group. For example: "It seems like people aren't hearing one another" or "I wonder if this topic is too complicated to address right before lunch." Once shared, it can be up to the group to decide whether the hypothesis rings true, and what they want to do about it (if anything).

- <u>Propose an action</u>: In some cases, I might give an instruction, such as "Let's take a break," or "Please exit down the fire escape and meet on the sidewalk until the fire department gives the 'all clear' signal."

- <u>Stay in awareness</u>: This may look like "doing nothing," but holding back and collecting more data can be a perfectly appropriate intervention.

To whit: I can think of situations in which a participant has said something inflammatory, perhaps with the unconscious intent of sidetracking a difficult conversation. In that moment, pretending that the comment never happened could be the best way to help the group avoid being derailed. (Of course, the opposite could be true.)

Even for an active facilitator, not everything you hear, see, or experience needs to be acknowledged, and not every problem is really a problem. As Calvin Coolidge said, "If you see ten troubles coming down the road, you can be sure that nine will run into the ditch before they reach you." Reflexively reacting to every comment or action makes the facilitator the center of attention, which is unproductive for the long-term health of the group. Over the course of any project, it's wise to let some of those "troubles" fall into the ditch without any action on your part.

Sometimes the way to be most helpful is really by doing nothing. Recently I facilitated a small team run by two well-meaning executives who kept stumbling over their distrust for one another. While discussing the organizational mission, the conversation veered away from the topic at hand and the two began ticking off one another's irritating habits. I could feel the tension suddenly start to rise.

But rather than guide them back to the planned topic, I let them keep sniping at each another. I took a few steps out of their line of sight and backed up against a far wall in the meeting room. I tried to make myself as invisible as possible, taking author Marvin R. Weisbord's advice, "Don't just do something, stand there!"

The executives kept going, laying out frustrations that had previously been unspoken. After a few tense minutes, the conversation swerved again. One said to the other, "I'm glad you told me. I didn't know that bothered you," and they both pledged to manage their interactions more carefully in the future.

It's difficult to know how and when to intervene, since any intervention could be focused on an individual, different sub-groups, or the entire organization. Choosing such a "level of system" for an intervention can be key to how your intervention lands, and what happens next.

Take the case of a meeting participant saying something inflammatory to the group. A leader could intervene at the individual level by calling out the person's behavior (e.g., "I found your use of that word to be upsetting and inappropriate.") This might work perfectly, generating new awareness for that person and curtailing the unproductive behavior without any discomfort. On the other hand, the intervention could land with a thud: The person could lash out, or others could escalate and expand the brewing conflict.

Or the facilitator could intervene at the group level with an observation like, "I notice that some people in the group have had a reaction to what was said." This approach is less confrontational, but it has its own risks. The facilitator could be seen as hanging meekly on the sidelines rather than addressing the issue forcefully.

In my practice, I try mightily not to man-splain or scold (though I'm not always successful). Most of my interventions tend to go down smoothly because I'm trying so hard to be gentle and not call out people directly for problematic behaviors. The downside of my low-friction approach is that I may be missing the opportunity to provoke new awareness and/or a meaningful exchange that could unlock something important for people in the group. And that's a potential loss: Provocation can be a powerful tool for any leader striving to add something to the group that otherwise doesn't exist.

Sometimes the way to add that missing element is through soothing encouragement and gentle support. At other times, it is through a kick in the pants. I ask myself,

"Which does my client need most in this moment – a blanket or sandpaper?"

In moments of trial and uncertainty, some clients may need a "blanket" to get through a painful situation, or to counteract raw feelings or low confidence. At other times, the client may be settling into unproductive habits or pushing back against needed changes. When people are stuck and oblivious, I might opt to provide "sandpaper" – a challenge, a discomfiting observation, or some other intentional irritation to reset the client's thinking and spur new insights.

Many consultants are reluctant to offer sandpaper for obvious reasons. We all want our clients to like us and be happy with our work. I also want them to pay me at the end, and then hire me back next time, and they won't do that if I spend all my time flipping over the tables and challenging every aspect of the status quo. As I learned early in my life, being genial and complimentary, smiling a lot, and saying nice things all tend to leave a good impression. People seem to like me more when I'm agreeable.

But my job isn't to be liked; it's to be helpful. Sometimes people need more than a soft touch to break out of a destructive pattern or acknowledge a misperception. Since groups and individuals all have unfinished business (usually around the avoidance of something painful) it can be enormously helpful to wield a discomfiting observation at a key moment.

I've learned how to be effectively provocative through sarcasm. In the mid-2010s I was working with a team that was enthusiastic about creating a physical library of books and magazines in the basement of their building at a time when nearly all information had already moved online.

This struck me as weirdly anachronistic, and I told them so. I ribbed them mercilessly for "building the last bricks-and-mortar library in North America." They were taken aback by my mocking critique, but they went ahead with their plans anyway. Maybe sandpaper wasn't the best choice in that moment.

Or, maybe what I did was just fine. It's possible that my power to influence their work was going to be limited no matter which approach I took. I've learned that there are limits to my influence, and that's fine. The client has to own their choices and their work, and I have to support them through whatever they might decide. After my client locked-in their library decision, I helped them figure out how to implement it.

Like everyone else in the world, my library-building clients had mental blocks and insecurities that, in this case, contributed to their making some odd planning choices. I took my shot at helping them see what I saw, but my snarky sandpaper comments weren't enough to dissuade them from the path they were taking.

And that's ok, because honestly, what do I know? Even though their plan seemed cuckoo to me, it's their plan, not mine. Maybe that initiative would transform their department and increase their influence within the organization. Maybe what the world really did need in 2010 was one more bricks-and-mortar library.

My job was to raise awareness of whatever I sense and observe and hypothesize that might help, and then let the client decide what deserves their attention. To them, my interventions are another set of data points that they can choose to hold or choose to set aside.

How you deliver your sandpaper moments matters; you have to balance enough roughness to get their attention, but not so much roughness that they turn you off. It's difficult to get the right mix of impact and sensitivity. I've come to learn that a few stems (which are essentially sentence-starters, like those Mad Libs fill-in books I used to devour as an adolescent) are invaluable tools. If I use these stems to start my sentences, I invariably end up making impactful statements in ways others can hear:

- *"I'm noticing..."* This is a useful stem for putting out raw data without imbuing any meaning to it. Example: *"I'm noticing several people speaking at once."*

- *"I'm curious about..."* This stem helps you own an observation without putting too much weight or value in it. It also reminds me to stay curious and avoid judgment. Example: *"I'm curious about why this topic is generating so much energy for you."*

- *"Help me understand..."* This stem can be used for even challenging observations. Example: *"Help me understand why everyone got quiet after Sasha made her comment."*

- *"I wonder..."* This is a great opening for a hypothesis, even a somewhat pointed one. Example: *"I wonder if everyone feels they've had an opportunity to speak to this issue...?"*

- *"I'm hearing..."* I use this to paraphrase others' comments or suggest a hypothesis. And it can be a subtle way to move a conversation onto a subtopic that people are otherwise ignoring. Example: *"I'm hearing lots of people talk about limits and endings, but not a lot about opportunities that might exist."*

- *"I heard you say..."* This is a great stem in emotionally charged moments when you want to be careful about being seen as putting words in another person's mouth. Example: *"I heard you say that this topic ought to be off-limits for our group."*

- *"This makes me think of..."* is a great way to insert an observation or personal insight into a discussion without hijacking it.

All interventions start with the intervener, but their value and import are in the eye of the beholder. If an intervention produces a beneficial effect, great! If it doesn't, try something else. Or, when all else fails, stand back and wait to see what happens next.

# Chapter 8

# The Paradoxical Theory of Change

*"Do you have the patience to wait till your mud settles and the water is clear? Can you remain unmoving until the right action arises by itself?"*

- Lao Tzu

A key role of any consultant is to make the client's work easier and more coherent, to help clients change and grow. But what's more difficult than changing and growing? We all have lots of barriers to overcome. Some people are unsure how to change. Others may know what to do, but don't know where to start. Or they can't motivate themselves to take the steps they know are required. If changing and growing were easy, we'd all be doing it ourselves and fancy consultants would be out of business.

Gestalt consultants have picked the lock that keeps people from embracing change. We know that change requires energy, and that energy can only mobilized through awareness. It's that formula I cited earlier in this book: Gestaltists raise awareness to mobilize the energy for change.

Even before my Gestalt training I did a version of this. When I'd first meet with a client, I'd ask a lot of questions, listen for disconnects, and comment on what I was hearing. In many cases, my initial inquiry would reveal confusion and mixed signals that nobody had noticed before. When the client saw this too, it produced an "aha!" moment that reframed the work and got everyone excited. My inquisitiveness and naivete had helped illuminate overlooked problems and generated enthusiasm to do things differently.

This pattern has helped build my career and kept my clients coming back over and over for more. When clients hire me they ask for help "writing a strategic plan," "building consensus," or "enhancing teamwork." But I know that the lasting value of my involvement comes from the questions and small observations that help people get unstuck.

Why does this work? Or better yet: Why weren't clients able to do any of this themselves? I may be good at my job, but I know that a big asset I possess is that I'm an outsider. The facilitator's stance with one foot in the group and one foot outside of the group gives me perspective, a bit of distance that keeps me from getting bogged down in too many details and preconceptions. I can see things that nobody else can simply because I'm looking in from a different angle.

But it's not just a matter of perspective. Lots of organizations spin their wheels and stay stuck because they focus on the wrong things. They are seduced by the future or mired in the past, without realizing that the seeds of change and growth are sown in the present.

# IMPACT

I understand why people make this choice. When engaged in planning, it seems to make sense to invest time fantasizing about the desired future state, and to create captivating visions of how things will be. And of course, some of this is necessary. You must have a picture of your destination if you ever hope to get there.

It also makes sense to look back at the past, to make sense of recent successes and challenges. It's the only way to build knowledge and wisdom for individuals and the group.

But thinking about the past and the future isn't nearly enough, and many people and organizations get the emphasis totally wrong. Gestalt practitioners know that they must focus resolutely on the present – the here and now – to unlock and unblock change.

Read that again: To facilitate growth and change, you must set aside the past and de-emphasize the future, and instead invest energy in understanding and fully inhabiting the present. It sounds nonsensical.

Therapist Arnold Beisser calls this the Paradoxical Theory of Change, a key element of the Gestalt approach. We know that change happens when we become more fully aware of who we are, not when we attempt to become different. Finding new understanding of the current state opens doors we didn't even realize existed and unleashes new energy for change.

These understandings of the current state don't need to be awe-inspiring mountains of new perception. Even modest insights about the "here and now" can have a huge effect. Dorothy Siminovich cites a Turkish expression: "Küçük ama büyük," or "small but big." As she explains in her book *A Gestalt Coaching Primer: The Path Towards Awareness IQ*, "A small piece of revealed awareness at the right moment is what ignites the most energy for new possibilities." Gestaltists know that a rock, a pebble, or even a tiny grain of sand can change everything.

That's why the formula for the Gestalt practitioner is cunningly simple: Raise clients' awareness of the present so they can mobilize energy for change in the future.

We know that we can't move ahead effectively without exploring and acknowledging the current moment and environment, but convincing ourselves or others to do so isn't easy. The future is often shiny and sparkly, and the present can feel mired with dreary problems and complications. There is a strong tendency to simply paper-over today's dull reality in favor of a glittering fantasy about the future. The flying cars of tomorrow are always more fun to contemplate than the crises of today.

The past has its own allure. We all hold regrets and emotions about things we've done or failed to do, and people can be unwilling to move ahead until those experiences are fully explored. For some unfortunate groups, relitigating the past can become an obsession that blocks out everything else.

And here's the biggest challenge with The Paradoxical Theory of Change: Investing our attention in the "here and now" seems counter-intuitive. And for organizations under intense pressure to get moving (which includes just about everybody), a focus on the present feels downright unnecessary. Plus, paradoxes are really, really hard.

But this paradox is true. I've seen it with my own eyes.

During my Gestalt training, I had the opportunity to meet leaders of the Hungarian Helsinki Committee, which works to protect the rights of the most desperate refugees in Hungary. This group had asked for help crafting a fundraising plan; while they were successful in fulfilling their mission, they had struggled to make and follow even the most basic plans they created for themselves. As Marta Pardavi, the Committee co-chair, told us, "We focus on the external with less attention to the internal," leaving their staff management and fundraising workflows in a constant state of disarray.

Our consultant team met with six members of the Committee staff, who spoke rationally and coolly about their work. Afterwards, we returned to our hotel and conferred about how to proceed. As we deliberated and debated, one member of our team unexpectedly started weeping, overcome with emotion about the Committee's work. After a few minutes of high emotion, she shared what was behind her sudden tears. She told us that despite the measured and logical ways the staff had spoken, she felt a well of deep sadness and despair below the surface that others had missed.

Frankly, this was confounding to me. My colleague's emotional reaction seemed beside the point, an unwelcome detour from what clearly needed to be done. I thought to myself, "What does this outburst have to do with a fundraising plan?"

But instead of setting aside our associate's raw emotional experience as a useless distraction, we were guided by our iGold faculty advisor Chantelle Wyley to stay with the emotional data and dig deeper. We hypothesized that perhaps the organization's culture prized rationality and cool logic so much that it didn't allow space for strong emotions, and that that blockage might seriously limit their ability to move past their current fundraising and management struggles. It felt like a perilous leap with a client we barely knew, but we were encouraged to take the risk and share our hypothesis.

So we returned the next day with a simple invitation: Rather than focus on their future fundraising plans as they had originally requested, we offered to meet individually with each leader to discuss the "here and now." We speculated that addressing the submerged emotional issues of the moment might help free the leaders to plan and implement more effectively. I could sense they were skeptical about our suggestion, but to my amazement they agreed to give it a try.

I had the opportunity to meet one-on-one with Ms. Pardavi for an hour-long discussion. We talked about how she experienced the pressure and anxiety, and how it affected her oversight of an under-resourced and besieged cadre of advocates working in a society that often expresses hostility towards the refugees they are dedicated to protecting.

I prompted her with gentle questions and listened carefully to her answers. I didn't offer advice or suggestions, but simply held the space for her to verbalize things she rarely if ever discussed. Our conversation felt intimate and real. As our time drew to a close, I helped her summarize a more compelling picture of how she was feeling, and how her emotions might matter to herself and others.

When we reconvened afterwards, Committee staff reported back on what they had experienced in their individual sessions. To a person, they shared that the confidential discussions had helped them see their situation more clearly, and that their new awareness had left them feeling energized in ways they hadn't expected. They felt rejuvenated. In just a few hours of interaction, we had helped them acknowledge to themselves the emotional toll of their profession and generate new energy to face those challenges together.

Years later, it appears that our brief intervention may have contributed to a beneficial shift in the leaders' attention. Four years later, in a profile in *Politico Europe*, Ms. Pardavi told a very different story than the cool and factual summary we had heard at our first consultant meeting. She told the journal that "one of the main challenges is ensuring the emotional well-being of her staff, which faces constant pressure from the government and its allies." Score one for Gestalt.

In my practice today, the Paradoxical Theory of Change reminds me to collect as much data as I can about the here and now, and to focus my client's attention on the present as well. It's not that we don't talk about the future or acknowledge the past; we just make sure we invest enough time and energy to fully embody the present before moving ahead.

Even simple interventions can produce powerful awareness and energy for clients. I recently started a meeting by inviting participants to share one word that described the issue we would be discussing. The result of this process was a revealing conversation about which descriptions were most common, which were surprising, and which were missing – and the attitudes and experiences that lay below. In a 30-minute check-in, the group realized new insights about the topic, which enabled them to see more clearly how they collaborate.

Doing so was neither a detour nor a delay of the real work; it was the work. Participants needed to get fully grounded in a shared figure of the present before moving on to consider the future. It reminded me of a Gestalt truism: "It's not the thing that matters; it's our relationship to the thing." Learning how participants hold the work in their hearts and minds is just as important and is often overlooked.

I acknowledge that many clients get impatient with such an approach, and some even try to "help" by urging me to move things along faster. They feel desperately driven to leap before looking. And in my absence, clients and groups would do just that – speed ahead without a full and shared picture of the present, and their haste would probably feel satisfying for a while. But soon the same old and frustrating patterns would likely re-emerge because everyone really isn't on the same page. These might include:

- A few strong personalities or influential leaders may dominate the conversation, while others are silent and/or distracted – in part because they aren't fully bought-in to the context of the discussion.

- Old questions and controversies might re-emerge awkwardly, long after they seemed to have been settled. When this happens, the conversational back-tracking can feel deeply irritating and dispiriting.

- The discussion may popcorn around from topic to topic without developing a clear flow, and without bringing questions to full resolution. The result can make the whole process feel like a pointless "debating society," a meandering bull session that leaves participants with the sense that "nothing got done."

It's one reason why many strategic plans never get implemented. By focusing prematurely on the future, groups fail to fully understand the present, which undermines their ability to work collectively to reach their goals. Lacking an awareness of the present, they are unable to sustain the energy they need to implement the changes they desire.

I typically raise my own awareness of the "here and now" by conducting confidential pre-process interviews that ask about the range of perceptions, opinions, beliefs, and attitudes that exist among participants. In addition to easing my entry into a new group, the interviews give me data about the multiple realities I might encounter, and they minimize the chances I'll be blind-sided by an unexpected issue.

There is tension between taking the time to explore the "here and now," and pervasive feelings of impatience and anxiety that define our work environment. Most clients I encounter believe it is impossible – or at least unwise – to slow down when there is so much to accomplish. They bristle at any attempt to move deliberately, so I try not to use phrases like "slow down." Instead, I try to tap the brakes by emphasizing the importance of establishing context and "assuring that everyone is up to speed." Sometimes this works.

I'm usually able to focus enough attention on the "here and now" to raise the client's awareness and mobilize new energy for change...but some participants' impatience is too much to overcome. A few years ago, I worked with an office at the World Bank that was struggling with poor coordination and a chronic inability to follow through on their aspirations.

Every year or two they had invested enormous time and energy in writing a new strategic plan, but then found that none of their exciting initiatives ever got off the ground. This mirrored the pattern at the highest levels of the organization, with each successive administration intent on remaking the bureaucracy in their image, rolling out an extensive new reorg and then shelving it before it was completed.

For my project, I worked closely with the department staff, an organizing team, and the group's vice president to lay out a day-long process that would build broader context and generate lasting consensus. But when the meeting day arrived, the leaders became so impatient with our agreed-to approach that they hijacked their own meeting.

The senior staff, who were accustomed to dominating conversations and getting their way, started voicing their discomfort almost immediately. I was told, "This is not how we run our meetings," and "You don't understand how we operate." As the complaints became louder, the vice-president took the microphone and announced that she was going to lead a plenary discussion of "the important stuff" – namely making elaborate plans for the future. Our agreed-upon agenda was set aside, and my role was reduced to taking notes and tracking time.

I learned in the months that followed that the group had fallen back into the same unproductive patterns they had experienced before. They lost interest in the plans they made that day and lost track of their exciting initiatives. By focusing on the future and rushing past the "here and now," they failed to build awareness and mobilize energy for change. By doing things the same way as always, they achieved the same results as always. Their approach kept them stuck, blocking the progress they wanted to achieve.

Here's another example of how a small insight about the "here and now" can spark powerful awareness and new energy. When coaching a trio of mid-level executives over several months I noticed two patterns of behavior: They almost always spoke in the same order (Person A, Person B, and then Person C), and they rarely addressed anything said by one another.

After I shared these observations, I waited. There was a long and very uncomfortable period of dead silence. Time seemed to screech to a halt.

After one leader spoke, I invited them to speculate on what the data might mean. They paused, and then began to really dig in. They got excited hypothesizing about what might be going on and why it might be happening. Newly energized, they began to debate and connect as they never had before. The ensuing discussion became one of the most spirited and productive of all the coaching sessions we conducted. Asked afterwards to describe the discussion, the most skeptical of the three called our conversation "invigorating."

I often see people struggling because they are lost in the past or lost in the future, rather than dwelling in the only place they have agency, which is in the present. Again Lao Tzu: "If you are depressed, you are living in the past. If you are anxious, you are living in the future. If you are at peace, you are living in the present."

Peace AND agency – that's what's possible when you can shift your attention to the "here and now." Example: One coaching client recalled to me how wonderful her job was before her company was acquired in a merger. She said she now feared about what could happen if she pushed back on a colleague who treated her disrespectfully.

I observed that her nostalgia for the past and fear of an imagined future were depriving her of the ability to move forward in the present. The past is done, I told her: Her old company no longer exists. The future hasn't happened: She has no idea how her co-worker will respond, or what she will say or do. Her power to bring about change only exists in the here and now, so that's where it makes sense for her attention to dwell.

I invited her to explore her current feelings, and her relationship with her colleague. I invited her to think about what she values in her career, and how she experiences her job today. And finally, I invited her to speculate on what kinds of actions she might take to improve her situation, and how those would feel. She said she left the conversation with new motivation to act on some long-standing challenges.

## IMPACT

The Paradoxical Theory of Change provides a proven path forward for any individual or group that feels stuck. Raising awareness of the "here and now" doesn't seem like it will be enough to get things moving in the right direction, but it often is. It's one of those paradoxes that proves itself to be true on repeated occasions. And it's in those moments when Gestalt shows its power and its magic.

# Chapter 9

# Holism, Complexity, and Levels of System

Many of us work with organizations comprised of complicated, confusing, and unpredictable humans acting erratically in situations that are inherently difficult to grasp. Thankfully, Gestalt offers three interconnected concepts that help any leader or consultant shed light on the environment and make meaning of what they're seeing.

The theory of *holism* suggests that most human systems function as wholes that are distinct from the mere sum of their constituent parts. Companies, teams, groups, and departments are complex organisms, the theory holds, that consist of many different and interconnected elements, all of which must be perceived together rather than simply as isolated components.

Gestalt calls attention to the whole of an organization... while also acknowledging that you can never truly perceive its entirety with clarity. To make things more complicated, going the other direction is also insufficient. As Gestaltists, we must retrain our minds to accept that what we are perceiving is both parts and a whole, without allowing one perception to push the other aside.

When we zoom in to see the trees, one picture comes into focus. Zoom out to see the forest, and different qualities emerge. We have to hold awareness of the parts even though doing so doesn't allow us to fully understand a system in its totality.

You could, for instance, examine the various departments within a company, but if you only looked at those individual parts you'd get a deeply flawed picture of the entire organization. A big company is more than its sales staff or its customer relations team, or any other of its myriad individual departments or functions. It's also the way those individual parts fit together, interact, and influence one another. It's more than the sum of its parts.

It isn't easy to do. People often have trouble distinguishing between dynamics that are local and unique to their section of the organization, and those that are shared more widely. And since they lack the wider perspective of the bigger picture, they can't see how what happens in one part can affect the others.

Holism doesn't insist that one must only see the forest or only see the trees, but rather that one's view of the trees and the forest is inextricably linked. Gestalt practitioners simultaneously hold both realities as valid and important.

When I begin collecting data about an organization, I know that characteristics I observe in one place will also be present elsewhere in some form or fashion. For instance, when working with a senior leadership of an NGO, I heard several officers complain that were uncertain about their own individual and collective roles in guiding the company. Later, when I talked with field staff and junior managers, I heard the same thing: They felt anxious because they didn't understand how their senior leaders were supposed to operate. I have no reason to believe the two groups conferred; I hypothesize that the friction felt in one part of the organizational body was simply observable in a different part of the body.

Holism even applies at a more granular level: It holds that people who are part of a system cannot be fully understood outside of that system. Individuals must be appreciated in their context.

Again, I know this from personal experience. Early in my career, I worked for a small consulting company whose president took an immediate shine to me. He found me brilliant and delightful, and his confidence boosted my own. I was quickly a star, and he mentored me in doing some of the best work of my life.

That is until he encouraged me to take a job with the large trade association that was our client. Whereas my consulting company was entrepreneurial and nimble, my new employer was bureaucratic and stodgy. I found the staid offices deadening and my bland co-workers stultifying. They didn't like me that much either. Without the enthusiastic support of my former boss, I lost confidence in my capabilities. My work life quickly devolved from being a joy to being an ordeal, and I became surly and unenthusiastic.

Which was the real me? The high-energy employee who could crank-out top quality product in record time, or the grumpy sourpuss unable to complete even simple tasks?

Of course, I was both the star and the goat. Had a Gestalt practitioner observed me in the consulting job they would have recognized that my excellence was not just intrinsic to me; I was also propped up by a vibrant environment that aligned with my personal style. My accomplishments were partly attributable to my skills, and partly attributable to my surroundings. And had that observer seen me at my association job, they would have understood that my low energy and insolence were brought into full bloom by my environment.

# IMPACT

When we feel under pressure or triggered by negative emotions in our midst (as I was at the association), we tend to close up. Creativity, trust, and morale are replaced by fear, resentment, cynicism, impatience, mistrust, jealousy, overwhelm, frustration, anxiety, disdain, or contempt. Our brain focuses on surviving rather than thriving.

In a safe and ordered environment, the opposite happens. Our emotional pendulum swings towards hope, compassion, opportunity, calm, pride, love, trust, and empathy. This is the kind of space where we sparkle!

Embedded in this concept of interconnectedness is a deep core of compassion. Since one can never truly understand another person's situation, one must strive to hold each individual as they present themselves, and without judgment. We don't understand the burdens that might push someone down and make them incapable at their job, or to behave in ways that may be unhelpful and damaging to the team.

So whenever a colleague struggles, the system itself must always shoulder some portion of the responsibility. And when someone is crushing it, some credit for their thriving must go to the supportive environment in which that person is operating.

In this way, Gestalt is inherently optimistic. Gestalt practitioners know that regardless of any challenges a person or group may have, each of us is naturally creative, resourceful, and whole. Our optimism leads us to look for systemic challenges that may undermine individuals' success and drag them into unproductive habits. And when we see that systems have failed, we look for ways to build agency and resilience among the people, because it's their individual successes that are crucial for the success of the team.

## Complexity

In common speech, we often use the words "complex" and "complicated" interchangeably, just as we also tend to mush together the terms "problem" and "dilemma." But each of these word pairs refer to fundamentally different things, so it pays to sort them out. If you approach a complex dilemma thinking it's merely a complicated problem (or vice-versa), you're likely to end up deeply frustrated with the results.

Problems can be vexing, but they can usually be solved by experienced people using models, strategies, and tools that are already familiar. Fixing the photocopier is complicated, but it can often be handled by a trained technician wielding a screwdriver and some circuit boards. Every vehicle built in the last twenty years is extremely complicated (the average car contains more than 30,000 separate parts, including more than 3,000 individual computer chips) but even the biggest repairs can usually be completed in a day or two, sometimes just by downloading new software. It's not rocket science.

How about jet science? While a jet aircraft is very complicated, taking it apart and putting it back together (carefully!) should produce the exact same set of physical outcomes – thrust, speed, lift, etc. – that allowed it to fly in the first place. A re-assembled aircraft should work exactly like the original because the interrelationships between the parts are predictable, as is the interaction between, say, a properly assembled wing and the air around it.

This is why a million enormous, massive, and complicated aircraft take flight every day without much incident. The reliability of their design, manufacture, and operation enables us to predict what would happen if you tinker with an aircraft's construction or fly it outside normal parameters. In the rare event of an accident, engineers can, with enormous precision, reconstruct an entire aircraft and reenact the sequence of events that led to the crash.

Complicated problems aren't necessarily small and contained. Problems can also be massive in scale and require enormous computational precision. NASA's scientists and engineers in the 1960s were world-class experts in their fields who invented new technologies in the course of their efforts, but they were mostly working with existing techniques and widely-accepted engineering methods that had been crafted years before.

To whit: NASA and its private sector contractors built the Apollo 11 rocket and calculated its course from Earth to the moon and back using hand-held slide rules, simple tools that had been in use since the 1620s. According to National Public Radio, these archaic instruments were critically important to one of the most transformative events in human history. Astronaut Buzz Aldrin said he "needed his pocket slide rule for last-minute calculations" during the harrowing final minutes as he and Neil Armstrong descended rapidly to the lunar surface. His low-tech computations allowed the first humans to land safely on the moon without running out of fuel or crashing into any giant lunar boulders.

In 2022, NASA used basic physics and lots of clever first-of-its-kind engineering to launch the James Webb Space Telescope, which included a mirror so large it couldn't fit inside the rocket. So they folded it up origami-style, and created a multi-stage system to deploy it once it arrived in a stable orbit in space. When the time came, the mirror unfolded perfectly as planned.

Their work was brilliant and ingenious – but the daunting challenges they overcame were merely complicated, not complex.

Larry Cuban, author of *How Can I Fix It: Finding Solutions and Managing Dilemmas* defines a problem as "a situation in which a gap is found between what is and what ought to be." The gap with the telescope was that nobody had ever unfolded a highly sensitive 21-foot-wide mirror a million miles from the Earth using remote control instructions. NASA figured out what ought to happen, and a way to make it so. And since the rules of physics and engineering are largely understood (at least at NASA), it went pretty much as planned.

Dilemmas, in contrast, are too gnarly for clean-cut resolutions. These are a special category of messy challenges where the none of the possible solutions are unambiguously acceptable, or maybe even achievable. Dilemmas incorporate a multiplex of forces occurring simultaneously that make it impossible to clearly link cause and effect. They may have features and characteristics that are constantly changing in unpredictable ways, with the inter-relationships between those pieces fluid and dynamic. And they usually involve unknowns and emergent qualities, so they can't be readily simplified or fully explained.

To transform the awesomely complicated deployment of the James Webb Space Telescope from a problem into a dilemma, NASA would had to have been operating in a universe in which the rules of physics and engineering were in a continual state of unpredictable flux. Thankfully, that wasn't the case.

Not sure if you have a dilemma or a problem on your hands? Lay out all the possible answers or solutions to the situation; if the best response you can come up with is "All of the above," or "None of the above," or "I'm not sure," or "Who knows?," or "Can we still think about this some more?" you're probably looking at a dilemma.

The social sciences are full of dilemmas, because these disciplines tend to deal with large numbers of people who act in contradictory, unpredictable, and counter-productive ways. Public health experts, for example, will spend the next fifty years unpacking how they could have prevented millions of Americans from rejecting a miraculous life-saving COVID-19 vaccine that had been successfully administered over ten billion times...in favor of a horse de-wormer. And how public health agencies ended up with less credibility on the topic than a bunch of bloggers and podcasters.

Criminologists and fans of TV's Law and Order franchise still debate the innocent prisoner's dilemma, in which a wrongly accused individual may have to falsely "admit" guilt to win parole (or a lesser sentence) or suffer a longer sentence for sticking to the truth.

Yes, this is flabbergasting. Our brains – which evolved to support us 50,000 years ago to live a simple life of hunting and gathering – haven't changed enough in the intervening years to make sense of this increasingly complex world we've created.

We are sophisticated enough to build an interconnected worldwide economy, but we are at a complete loss when something goes wrong. What should we do when supply chains get broken, when prices drop, or a population ages and becomes less productive? We've created the Internet but can't figure out how to keep the benefits of social media without destroying our social cohesion. We've built a complex web of hub-and-spoke airline flights that completely collapses when confronted with commonplace hazards like snow, wind, or fog.

Every day, the news is full of complex human-designed systems confronting powerful dilemmas. How can we maintain both privacy and security? How can we stimulate prosperity and growth while protecting the environment? How can we support independence while sharing responsibility for things we all value? Do more guns make us safer, or less safe? Do nuclear weapons keep the peace or make death and destruction more likely? Should we construct more nuclear power plants to save us from climate change if they also create a giant toxic dump of radioactive waste that will remain deadly for 250,000 years? Does building a new road ease congestion, or cause it?

Like paradoxes, dilemmas make my head hurt.

You can expect to see complexity in any human system, such as a company or a department, which makes it very difficult to know how to act. You could remove an engine from an aircraft in flight (but please don't!) and accurately predict the result. What happens if you remove one problematic person from a functioning team?

Things might get better, but since the people who remain in the organization may have subtle or dramatic responses to the removal, the resulting environment might be affected in completely unpredictable ways. For example, those who remain might resent the removal and make things worse.

The departing individual might "disappear" from the organization, or they might linger as a memory, an outside critic, a confidant to current employees, a competitor, or a phantom "lesson" to others that takes on a variety of meanings in different people's minds. Or, the remaining staff might compensate for the departure of their colleague as if nothing happened, resulting in no apparent difference at all.

Because human systems are inherently complex, it's essential to set aside any expectations for "solving problems" and instead look for ways to "manage dilemmas." Single interventions (such as firing that problematic employee) almost certainly won't lead to a miraculous change; the only sure thing is that there are no magic bullets.

Often, you won't be able to link causes to effects, since they can emerge in different spaces at different times. And actions and results may be wildly disproportional. The 80-20 rule posits that 80% of the significant outcomes in a system can be attributed to 20% of the interventions...but which ones?

Still, one can lead and manage in the chaos of a dilemma by letting go of what cannot be explained or controlled. The wise leader focuses less on articulating a fixed destination or rolling-out unalterable initiatives, and instead focuses on setting a clear direction for the group to aim towards.

It matters how you start, and how you stand. Start by investing in research, because the environment may have changed in significant but imperceptible ways since the last time you looked. Engage with a wide range of stakeholders in crafting your strategies, because hearing more voices enables you to collect more data before making meaning of it.

Some leaders convene a kind of Brain Trust, bringing together a diverse set of stakeholders for the purpose of airing divergent viewpoints, challenging stale thinking, and developing awareness of unexpected dynamics. By opening themselves to confusing data, these leaders limit the chances of "groupthink," the tendency to make non-optimal decisions spurred by the urge to conform to established patterns of action.

And once your initiative launches, it's wise to view it with modesty. I advise my clients to hold their work lightly, framing all actions as exploratory, incremental, and tentative. Doing so enables them to test many ideas at once, collect data on their impacts, and quickly kill lines of action that aren't working or performing to expectations. Failure, instead of being a sign of incompetence, becomes an essential and repeatably useful tool for success.

This approach has been central to the Agile software development methodologies popularized in Silicon Valley and adopted by many other industries in the past twenty years. Journalist James Surowiecki has posited that Agile's ethos of "fail fast, fail often" is now the tech industry's mantra. According to Google's Dr. Astro Teller, "The question is how and how fast can you discover that the thing you're working on is the wrong thing to be working on"...so you can move your focus on to something more productive.

Sharing and adopting this fail-fast mindset is a central tenet in the management of chaotic situations and complex dilemmas. And the Agile approach has been very valuable in the tech sector, but I don't run my clients through that rigid kind of step-by-step process. That's far too much "process" and not enough "people" for my taste.

Rather, I go back to my Gestalt ideals, helping raise clients' awareness of the unique kinds of chaos and complexity that exist in their environment. Then I support them in identifying and letting go of unproductive patterns of behavior. This helps mobilize the whole team's energy for actions that will build on strengths that already exist within themselves and their organization.

## Levels of System

The Gestalt practitioner must open her/his lens to perceive both the big and the small, the individual pieces and the entirety of organization, and then guide our clients to do the same. As I noted earlier in the chapter, we must see both the forest and the trees, while also noticing the relationship among the parts and their connection to the whole. It's a lot to take in.

One way to bring order to this chaos is take note of the levels of the system, starting with the individual. Every organization is constructed by and consists of individual people, and the perceptions, opinions, beliefs, and attitudes that guide their behavior. Those individuals tend to work in teams, groups, departments, or task forces, each of which also represent levels of the same system. In bigger organizations, those groupings may be aggregated into larger systems, such as offices, divisions, or affiliates, which may be all linked together into an even larger corporate system. Several corporations may be thought of as an industry or sector, and the aggregated sectors can be grouped into an economy.

Effective interventions take note of all the levels of the system. Ineffective interventions try to make change by only acknowledging the importance of some of those levels of system. In my field, this is what I call "system level error," and it's shockingly pervasive.

The most typical system level error is to try to make change by intervening at the top of the organizational pyramid, and then expecting all the other subordinate levels of system to just fall in line.

I've seen this pattern of "top down" change management fail on many occasions, even in relatively small organizations. A few years ago, I worked with a for-profit company that provides refugee relief services under contract to the US government. With an impending change of presidential administrations, the company's COO foresaw a challenging economic environment ahead, so he quickly developed a bold plan to reorganize the company's departments and diversify their revenue streams. He rallied support from the CEO and the six department heads, then rapidly won the approval of the Board of Directors.

# IMPACT

What the COO had failed to do was engage the front-line employees or middle managers in the process of analyzing the situation or devising the reorganization plan. So when the package of far-ranging organizational and structural changes was announced at a mandatory staff meeting, it came as a profoundly unwelcome surprise to almost everyone in attendance.

Instead of seeing this as a rescue plan designed to save the company, people reacted with shock, fear, resentment, and anger. Why, people wanted to know, was this extreme degree of change necessary? Am I going to lose my job? Are we going out of business? And if I am not being fired, what are my new responsibilities? Who will my boss be? How will any of this even work??

In retrospect, this reaction might have been expected.

While many of us perceive ourselves as independent, autonomous, and powerful, in fact we are all deeply influenced by the systems in which we are embedded. Every organization we join changes us, just as we change it. Every identity we embrace affects us, and every cause we champion leaves its mark. Everyone one of us is defined in part by the systems that include us, and each of those systems are affected in turn by our presence.

For the Gestalt practitioner, this means that if you notice a pattern of behavior in one level of the system, you can surmise that it might well be present in other levels as well. For instance, after every meeting I held with the executive director of a national healthcare advocacy organization I found myself feeling more confused than I had been before the conversation started. I always listened intently as he spoke, but I found the same result after every discussion: I couldn't make heads or tails about what he was saying.

Over time, I came to realize that he was dumping useless information on me because he was too overwhelmed to distinguish between what was important and relevant to the work, and superfluous trivia. He even told me the organization had several "top priorities," which pulled me up short.

Several top priorities? Was there ever a clearer sign that I was talking to someone with no ability to prioritize?

As you might imagine, he wasn't the only one in this large and diverse organization who had the same problem. As I started convening with his subordinates, I found that every one of them was deeply buried in projects and reports. They felt continually as though they were falling behind and couldn't focus. The leader's overwhelm and inability to prioritize was like a virus that had spread throughout the entire company.

When helping implement change, it pays to take note of every level of system in an organization, not just the levels that are easy to see and easy to reach. Each level is connected and interrelated, so one must strategize changes at multiple levels to support and amplify (rather than interrupt and short-circuit) the changes you seek.

I've noticed a tendency for leaders to attempt group-wide interventions when individual interventions might be more appropriate and effective. It's a common pattern. I remain irritated by a grade school teacher who couldn't figure out how to discipline one or two misbehaving students effectively, so she punished the entire class. The injustice and irrationality of her approach still rankles me fifty years later. (Talk about holding a grudge!)

In one of my former jobs, the executive director was reluctant to sanction a small group of employees for unprofessional behavior, so he issued new restrictive rules that affected the entire association. In both cases, the broad-brush interventions produced confusion and consternation. The "offenders" seemed to get off the hook for their actions, and everyone else suffered...an approach that generated considerable resentment.

Recently, a former client asked for help with a newly promoted executive who was having difficulty fulfilling the responsibilities and expectations of his job. In response, the CEO wanted to hold a leadership retreat to build better camaraderie among the team. I was eager for the gig, but I cautioned her about a glaring mismatch: While the retreat might be useful and fun, it would do little to address the problem she was trying to solve, which was how to support a new executive who likely needed individualized training and management.

The CEO had chosen a group intervention when an individual intervention was more appropriate. She aimed her attention at one level of system when the problems were elsewhere, and in doing so she was setting herself up for disappointment. Any consultant or leader must remain alert to these kinds of level-of-system errors and keep the focus where the impact will be greatest.

# Chapter 10
## Working with Boundaries

I was fortunate years ago to work with a consortium of advocacy organizations, each headed by a smart and competent leader. Individually, each was charming, capable, and dedicated, but the three leaders shared a vexing shortcoming: They had enormous difficulty managing their boundaries, and the pattern showed up repeatedly in almost everything they did.

The clients assembled a cadre of experts to develop breakthrough ideas...and then (rather than embrace the expert ideas they had purchased) repeatedly promoted their own approaches. They did the same with me: They hired me for my expertise in designing and facilitating meetings...and then ignored my professional judgment on how to design and facilitate meetings. When questions arose about an agenda I drafted, they didn't ask me about it (which would have taken 30 seconds to resolve). Instead, they debated among themselves in a convoluted email exchange that took a day to untangle.

The three leaders had difficulty differentiating their roles from one another. All three participated in every one of our planning calls, and then overlapped, contradicted, and distracted one another as we talked. When an issue emerged that needed resolution, I was never sure who I should call to sort things out.

They also had difficulty managing time boundaries. They scheduled 30-minute planning meetings that ran for more than an hour, and hour-long meetings that lasted nearly two. And since meetings didn't end on time, subsequent meetings also didn't start on time. Sessions were usually unstructured, with no defined leader or agenda. I often was invited to join a call without much idea about why we were gathered or how I was expected to contribute. And they had difficulty managing conclusions: Decisions that were made on one day could be relitigated or un-made on the next.

The result of all this chronic boundary mismanagement was an extra layer of chaos and anxiety for everyone involved. I know I felt it!

Boundaries matter. We understand this intuitively in the real world, where borders and boundaries create a sense of coherence and identity by marking the extent of countries and states. These lines, created by kings and presidents, wars, tradition, language, and culture, often hug bodies of water and scale mountain peaks, or trace measures of longitude and latitude.

And it's easy to recognize these as human constructs: If you climbed across the Andes you know you would not see a squiggly line separating Chile and Argentina. The line only exists because humans say it exists.

That fact doesn't negate its importance. National boundaries describe the limits of each country's authority and contribute to our sense of cultural and historical identity. Since we all act as though that squiggly line in the Andes really is there (and we might put fences and armies at our borders to enforce its existence), it might as well be there in fact.

Humans use boundaries to pull similar things together, and to distinguish between things that seem dissimilar. People who all speak a similar language and share a common culture tend to group together and separate themselves from people who sound and act differently.

We are a species intent on lumping and splitting. We created a single category called "dogs" to lump together the tiny Lhasa Apso and the giant St. Bernard. And while a German Shepherd may be the same size as a wolf, we split the two in our minds to acknowledge the difference between a domesticated animal that will sleep contentedly at your feet, and a wild and dangerous predator.

We use boundaries to help us organize our thinking and make sense of the world. It's a skill that helped ancient human species sort dangerous situations from benign ones, but our perceptions can mislead us. According to William H. Prescott's *History of the Conquest of Mexico*, when Tlaxcalan fighters first encountered conquistador Hernan Cortés on horseback in 1519, they saw one entity, possibly controlled by the horse's enormous head.

Such category errors can be costly, because when we misread the boundaries of a situation we will likely prescribe the wrong intervention. Hence the Parable of the Red Car: A man crosses a street and is nearly struck by a red car. The erroneous lesson he draws is that red cars are dangerous. The next day he crosses the same street and scrupulously avoids all red cars...only to be struck by a green car.

Boundary setting is also culturally specific. Since the Enlightenment, most westerners (like me) place ourselves as distinct systems at the center of our own environment. We hold "the self" to be the basis of reality (with everything else seen as being in relation to it), but this is not the only way. Buddhists see the self merely as "a temporary phenomenon, a nonpermanent combination of matter and mental/spiritual functions." For Buddhists, it is possible for the ocean to join the drop.

# IMPACT

Western culture has for centuries clung to a set of binary generalizations and boundaries that no longer make sense and can cause real harm. Most Americans think we can definitively and intuitively discern who is "black" and who is "white," even though those deeply-held definitions are fluid, inconsistent, and entirely fabricated. There is no scientifically valid definition of race, and the concept does not exist on a genetic level.

Similarly, who and what determines whether a person is male or female? What are the boundaries of heterosexual or homosexual? Don't look to science for answers: Scientists can't even agree on a clear delineation between being alive and being dead.

These boundaries themselves are neither intrinsically good or bad, but their effects may be. A physical boundary (like a fence) can imprison or restrict, but once you know where a line is drawn, it can have the paradoxical effect of liberation and empowerment within those bounds.

It is said that creativity loves a boundary. Great art forms like haiku and the sonnet feel more meaningful because they adhere to traditionally strict boundaries of meter, topic, and length. And we are often thrilled when an art form explores its boundaries and transcends them...which would be impossible if the boundary didn't exist in the first place.

Many boundaries in the business world are easy to perceive. This thing over here is McDonalds, and that gigantic thing over there is Walmart. Many of them put huge labels on their buildings to help us tell the difference.

And inside the big corporate boundary, many internal boundaries exist. A company might have divisions, departments, or stores – the kinds of distinctions that show up on org charts and office plans, guidelines that make those boundaries easy to see too.

While boundaries like these are obvious, others are rather obscure. In those cases, you might not know a boundary exists until you cross it.

# IMPACT

Years ago, I invited a friend from out of town to join me at my local Washington, DC gym while I played squash. When I came downstairs after my game I was surprised to find him running shirtless on a treadmill, and I embarrassedly told him to quickly cover up since this was a violation of the club's rules. He often ran shirtless on the street, so he couldn't imagine why this would be different...and I didn't think to tell him beforehand to keep his shirt on because I just assumed everyone already knew the rule. The only way to discover that a boundary existed between "behavior that is acceptable in one place" and "behavior that is unacceptable in another place" was by transgressing it.

Here's another: There is a man in my neighborhood who walks down the street singing loudly to the music playing in his headphones. I find this appalling (in part because his voice isn't very good); I strongly believe that one should only sing at full voice in the street when the music is audible to others. The man with the headphones draws the boundary of "where and how it's acceptable to sing loudly" in a very different place.

Invisible and unexpected boundaries can be just as meaningful as the obvious ones. In some situations, the "hidden" boundaries may be more important.

For example, there may be a group of female employees in an organization who share a commitment to promoting qualified women up the corporate ladder, and who are always looking for ways to boost the career prospects of women they encounter. For ambitious women, this "hidden" boundary may be a boon; for ambitious men, it may be seen as an unexpected obstacle.

Or a company may have employees who were "acquired" during a merger, and who still share a unique set of experiences or allegiances; they may continue to see themselves as a subgroup within the larger organization by virtue of their shared history or values. I saw this when I worked with the pharmaceutical giant Teva, which years after its merger still had employees who self-identified as "Actavis people." When internal challenges arose, the

Actavis people conferred, shared intelligence, and tried to align their coping strategies in ways the rest of their colleagues could never see.

When I start working with a new group, I pay attention to all sorts of boundaries:

- Time boundaries: Do events and activities start or end as planned? How much time is devoted to an activity? Which tasks get allotted the most time, and which get the least? Which things come first, and which are habitually put off to last? Some cultures are meticulous about starting and ending times, and others are much more relaxed. If you want to find out which you're in, show up late and see what happens.

- Functional boundaries: How are teams and divisions organized? Are all the people who work together on the same thing (e.g., sales) assigned to the same department or are they sprinkled around the organization?

- Role boundaries: How are roles and responsibilities allocated, and how well are their boundaries defined? Who speaks first, and who speaks last? Do multiple people discover themselves working on the same things without one another's knowledge, or are tasks left undone because they've fallen into the gaps?

- Personal boundaries: How do people define, observe, and enforce appropriate amounts of physical and emotional distance?

- Mission boundaries: Does the team have a clearly defined understanding of what work it will do, and what should be left to others?

- Resource boundaries: How are time, energy, and other resources allocated? What gets staffed, and what doesn't? What gets funded and what doesn't? Whose ideas spark investment, and which get discarded?

- Decision boundaries: To what extent does the group decide and move on? Are decisions flexible or firm? Is there a tendency to re-open and re-argue decisions over and over?

We know what good boundaries look like: They are the ones that enable the organization and its people to thrive and support their shared mission. As a Gestalt practitioner, I look for boundaries that are

- Permeable, allowing appropriate people, ideas, and other resources to move freely without being needlessly blocked. If vital information can't pass readily from one functional group to another, departments get siloed and communication and collaboration suffer. At a company like Amtrak, the sales team must be able to tell the food service department that ticket sales are up, and they should stock more food in the Café Car. And you want every employee to have the ability to quickly alert security if they see a suspicious package. But that permeability must also have limits: Amtrak doesn't want its accounting staff directing train engineers to cut corners on safety in a quest to save money.

- Navigable, meaning that it takes an appropriate amount of time and energy to cross a boundary, but not a herculean effort to do so. This is a place where many big organizations struggle. All bureaucracies tend to develop defenses designed to keep people and ideas out, even if that impulse runs counter to their larger mission. And in the case of resource boundaries, budgets must be both firm and flexible, allowing leaders just enough leeway to modify their plans when a critical need emerges.

- Clear and visible, meaning that the boundary is apparent to everyone and easy to define. Vague boundaries will get transgressed by people who can't see them. That can create a sense of chaos and unfairness if the penalty for crossing an invisible boundary is too harsh. Hard-to-see boundaries also breed reliance on "back door" sources of information and "special relationships," which privilege the powerful and knowledgeable and disadvantage everyone else.

- <u>In good repair</u>: Because boundaries are created by people and people who are constantly in flux, the boundaries they create are ever-changing...so they must be regularly maintained and tended. Boundaries must be flexible, so archaic requirements can be pushed aside when they stop making sense. On the other hand, too much change can be disorienting and counterproductive, leading people to wonder what rules and norms will be enforced from day to day. And if boundaries are ignored altogether, organizations may experience "mission creep," a slow and un-noticed distortion that can lead people to waste energy on things that don't align with the team's intended purpose.

- <u>Appropriate</u>: An organization should have only the boundaries it needs, and nothing more. Inappropriate or excessive boundaries create false narratives that divide and confuse, making people less effective, and the environment less fair. For years, the US armed forces barred women from combat positions, and prohibited LGBTQI service members altogether, but to what strategic end? Eventually, political and military leaders removed these boundaries, acknowledging that these distinctions didn't support its mission, and in fact detracted from it.

Being able to see boundaries gives the Gestalt practitioner numerous lenses through which to make meaning of what's going on. We know that boundaries are necessary and valuable, and that their management is key to operation of a healthy organization.

# Chapter 11

# The Unit of Work

Sometimes an extremely modest realization can be the most impactful. As I noted in earlier chapters, seeing something small and simple in a slightly new way can change one's entire perspective.

You might think of an effective Gestalt intervention as a series of these tiny flickers of insight about something that had been there all along, but had remained unnoticed or unarticulated. Taken alone, these sparks seem banal and inconsequential, and can be easily overlooked until they build into a blinding flash that shifts perspective, raises new awareness, and unleashes energy for change.

Here's one such tiny flicker of insight: Everything has a beginning, middle, and end.

Full stop.

# IMPACT

This little idea is called the Unit of Work, and that's pretty much all there is to it: Everything has a beginning, middle, and end.

The Unit of Work is small but mighty. It's an incredibly useful construct that can tame the blur of activity swirling around us by chunking it down into coherent bites.

It's easiest to see the Unit of Work in mundane examples, but it can refer to any clearly bounded and understandable experience, project, event, or initiative. Every narrative we've heard, every book we've read, and every movie we've seen has a beginning, middle and end. The meal you just ate had a beginning, middle, and end. So did your last vacation. Our relationships have a beginning, middle, and end – and so do our lives. You can think of a Unit of Work as a little high-level story about anything that can or did or will happen.

| **Unit of Work** | | |
|---|---|---|
| Beginning | Middle | End |

It's a seductive model in part because our brains are naturally drawn to threes. Three Little Pigs. Three Blind Mice. Three Wise Men. Our attraction to groups of 3 is not random. Patterns are always easier to remember than an unstructured sequence of events or facts. It just so happens that three is the smallest number required to create a pattern.

And the compartmentalization aspect of the Unit of Work also feels satisfying, familiar, and coherent. It's as if there are three buckets just sitting there waiting for us to classify anything and everything we experience into its beginning, middle, and end.

At this point you may reasonably ask, "So what?"

Well. The Unit of Work framework can point us to problems we might otherwise not be able to perceive by helping distinguish between moments that are well-structured and those that are not. When a Unit of Work feels satisfying, it's likely because its beginning, middle, and end were each fully realized.

Think of the most memorable movie you've ever seen. The filmmaker likely started by introducing you to the setting and characters. In the middle there was a conflict or quest. In the end there was some sort of resolution that leaves us with a feeling of closure. When all three elements have been adequately addressed, you can sense it.

Conversely, when a Unit of Work lacks a coherent beginning, middle, or end you can intuitively feel some sort of absence or imbalance. I've seen plenty of movies that failed at the beginning to adequately explain the premise or flesh-out the characters into real and recognizable people. Other movies I've seen became convoluted and confusing in the middle, failing to stitch together their disparate pieces and pay off their initial set-up. Despite those films' charms, I have walked out of many such theaters feeling deeply "meh."

And lots of narratives fail at the end to resolve the story in a satisfying way. Sometimes this lack of closure is intentional (as in movies like *Lost in Translation*), an artistic choice designed to leave us disquieted. But often it's just poor writing. The hit TV series *Lost* ran on ABC starting in 2004, and during its six years on the air it introduced numerous supernatural mysteries, many of which were left unresolved from episode to episode. When the show finally wrapped in 2010, viewers expected some clear and satisfying answers to the confusing and nonsensical plot twists they had watched...which they didn't get. *Lost's* writers had thrown a raft of weird story lines in the air seemingly for no reason other than to shock and confuse. In the end, they couldn't come up with a fulfilling way to explain what all the craziness meant, and many in its audience felt burned.

Let's bring this back to the work world: Kurt Lewin, considered the father of social psychology and one of the leading originators of Gestalt, created a Change

Management Model in the 1940s to describe and manage complex transition processes.

Lewin saw change in three distinct phases: Unfreeze, when the patterns of the status quo loosen and become less solid. It's in this stage that people let go of their attachments to the current environment; Change, when attitudes and habits alter to accommodate new circumstances; and Re-freeze, when norms harden into a new fixed reality. In other words, the process of change is a Unit of Work that has a beginning, middle, and end.

The same can be said about any well-run meeting. The beginning is about getting started, setting context, and aligning everyone around a set of tasks. The middle may be somewhat chaotic, as participants put forward different ideas about what matters, or how to think about their options. The end of the meeting is when you press for resolution, summing up what's been decided (and what hasn't), and mapping out next steps.

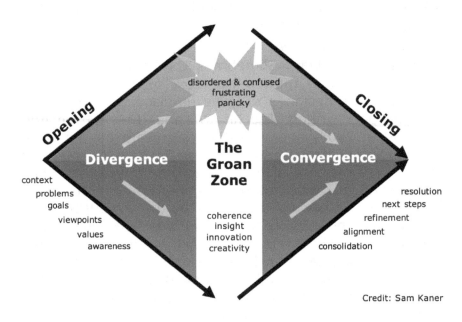

Credit: Sam Kaner

This looks a lot like the Diamond Participation Model created by consultant Sam Kaner, who slices his process into five stages that align well with the Unit of Work. In the beginning, there is the introduction of the issues at hand and exploration of divergent points of view. As I mentioned in Chapter 5, in the middle is the Groan Zone, a period of confusion, uncertainty, and irresolution; while painful, this is the time when new ideas and creativity can emerge. Finally, the successful meeting ends with convergence and alignment, followed by closure.

Kaner's model is reassuring and useful, but it only really applies to meetings. The Unit of Work is an all-purpose model that can be applied to everything.

And because Units of Work can be nested inside one another and/or can overlap, they can be used for very granular analysis. The beginning of an activity has a beginning, middle, and end. The middle has a beginning, middle, and end. And the end has a beginning, middle, and end. And each of those subsets has a beginning, middle, and end. One could continue to drill down (or zoom up) to think about these as the "beginning of the beginning" or the "middle of the end" for as long as such insights continue to have value.

This granularity is especially helpful for large endeavors that involve multiple steps and phases, possibly over a long period of time. You might think of a whole project as a Unit of Work, each of the phases as a Unit of Work, and each of the meetings or subsidiary activities as nested Units of Work, each with a beginning, middle, and end.

| Unit of Work | | |
|---|---|---|
| Beginning | Middle | End |
| **Unit of Work** | **Unit of Work** | **Unit of Work** |
| Beginning  Middle  End | Beginning  Middle  End | Beginning  Middle  End |

Because it's so simple and intuitive, I've found myself using this framework to ground myself when events seemed to be spinning around me. I can easily explain the Unit of Work to clients, and they can readily understand how to use it.

I often use the model to keep impatience in check. I worked recently with a panel of media executives considering changes to a national funding formula, a fraught six-month process intended to balance the wide-ranging and divergent needs of hundreds of stakeholders by reallocating millions of dollars. From the start of our work together, the client and panelists were extremely anxious to come up with the "correct" formula, even before they'd had a chance to review detailed financial data or learn about one another's interests and needs.

They were eager to jump to the end of their assigned Unit of Work – the final revision of the funding formula – without going through the beginning and middle. So a large part of my intervention was helping them stay in the beginning and middle, resisting the temptation to jump ahead to the end. At the start of each monthly meeting, I would re-iterate my perception of where we were in the process (beginning, middle, or end), and what a group in that phase of its work might be likely to experience.

At the start, I acknowledged participants' anxiety, eagerness, and energy, while inviting them to accept the pace of the process, take time to get to know one another so they could build trust, and to learn what issues really matter to themselves and their colleagues. In the middle, I reassured participants that even though some might experience despair at this point, confusion, uncertainty, ambivalence, and impatience were normal during this phase. Worry, I told them, is not a sign of failure.

And at the end, I acknowledged their desire to wrap things up quickly and move on to their next responsibilities; but instead of blazing through closure, I encouraged them to take stock of what they'd learned and accomplished, and to appreciate the contributions of those with whom they'd served. Several participants credited this framing as crucial in helping them keep their expectations and emotions in check.

And since each meeting was its own Unit of Work, I paid attention to its beginning, middle, and end too. I made sure we always took time at the start of each meeting to check-in on what was new or present for participants at that particular moment. The middle of the meeting usually included the sharing of new data, and activities to make meaning of what had been presented. And we also concluded each session by inviting panelists to reflect on what they had learned, and identify issues or questions that had the most energy for them.

I don't think I ever said the words "Unit of Work" out loud to this group, but I held the model in my mind to remain grounded and support others in staying engaged. While approaching the sixth and final meeting, their confusion and uncertainty started to clear, and the panel landed on a funding formula that met the needs of the entire national network. We arrived at that destination by staying calm and remaining patient, and allowing time to explore options without jumping too quickly to unwarranted conclusions.

As we wrapped up our work together, some on the panel expressed amazement at this rapid coming-together, which took place seemingly without their notice. After feeling lost and uncertain for so many months, the group's sudden ability to coalesce without rancor around a well-supported resolution felt to them like some kind of magic.

Of course it wasn't magic; it was Gestalt. We succeeded together by paying attention to several concepts, including the Unit of Work.

In any process, beginnings are a time for setting context, establishing expectations, and acknowledging who is and isn't present. At the start, every participant wants to know the answers to some pretty basic questions:

- What are we doing? What's the purpose of this effort, and what will a successful outcome look like? What's the extent and limits of our authority? (e.g., are we deciding, advising, exploring…or something else?)

- Why are we doing this? What do we need to know about decisions or previous activity that have led us to this point?

- Why am I here (instead of somebody else), and what's my role? How will I be expected to perform, and what should I be contributing? Oh, and why are these other people here too (instead of somebody else)?

- What kind of resources will we have at our disposal? This includes how much time we're committing over what period, plus funding, staff support, and any other tools that will make the work possible. Also, what other information or insights can we get to help us navigate effectively?

The middle is the crunch-time where the really hard work often takes place, and it's crucial here to be both patient and compassionate. This is time for assembling and sharing data, making meaning, setting priorities, and exploring options. As I've noted elsewhere, this stage can feel both exhilarating and demoralizing in turns as people can disagree about everything, and emotions can get raw – which is why Sam Kaner dubbed it "the Groan Zone."

When handled poorly, this phase can feel even worse: If you haven't successfully explored basic questions during the beginning stage, unresolved points of confusion can re-emerge unexpectedly and grind progress to a painful halt.

Ends are when the work comes to resolution, and the team acknowledges what has been completed, what questions or tasks remain undone, and what actions or steps will follow. It's also the moment to acknowledge and celebrate individual and collective accomplishments, and recognize the contributions of those who made this moment possible.

When groups and leaders express impatience to jump ahead (which is often!), I find they most often scrimp on Beginnings and Ends. The most common errors I've seen are

- At the Beginning: Failure to set context. Some leaders have poor insight into how little their subordinates know or understand about the big picture in which they operate. So they launch new projects without sharing vital information that's in their head about why the work matters and the potential costs of failure or benefits in success. When this happens, group members may go along because they feel they have to, but with less energy. At some point the ambiguity can become unbearable for some people, and it can break through to the surface with irritation: "Tell me again why we're doing this??"

- At the Beginning: Failure to define the team. It pays to explain from the start why each participant is included in any given project team, and what each person is expected to contribute. People want to know: Who has been included, who has been excluded, and why? How will we function together? How will we facilitate and maintain trust? How will we communicate? How will we collaborate?

- At the Beginning: Failure to define the group's task (and especially its authority). To the extent possible, leaders must define what mission the group is assembled to complete – and a key element of that is the degree of authority they will have. Is this group intended brainstorm, hypothesize, recommend, sign-off, or decide? There is no shame in a leader saying, "I just want your ideas, but in the end the decisions will be mine to make" – but I've heard many clients express real reluctance to articulate such a clear and unambiguous goal.

- At the End: Failure to close the process. Some groups and processes tend to run on and on, with the original end point being extended or redefined ad infinitum. When this happens too frequently, participation may drop to the point that the group has "withered on the vine," continuing to exist but no longer accomplishing much...or even convening. Such a lingering death can color people's perceptions of the entire experience, making them overlook earlier progress and see the whole process as less successful than it might actually have been.

- At the End: Failure to acknowledge successes and contributions. Being thanked and respected is essential to maintaining relationships and energy. So it's surprising how many work projects end without any acknowledgement of individual or collective contributions.

I've seen all of these breakdowns in my years as a consultant. For example, I worked with a coalition of advocates planning a 100-person symposium for researchers and medical professionals. The organizers created a detailed agenda but had no shared understanding of what they wanted to accomplish. They had no plan for helping participants get grounded in the topics they would cover. They allotted no time at the end of the two days for people to make meaning of what they would learn. And they had no idea what, if any, follow-up would occur.

Like most clients, this group of smart and well-intentioned people had hired me because they wanted to help their participants go through the middle part of the process, where they would converge on exciting ideas. What the organizers lacked was an awareness that their session also needed a fully-realized beginning, and a clear and intentional end.

When I was newer in my profession, I might have tried to facilitate the agenda as they had written it. I might have had doubts about their approach, but I was much more willing to just let them chart the course and hope for the best.

Now I see that my job as a Gestalt practitioner isn't to simply provide what my clients ask for; it's to help them be more successful. They hired a consultant to facilitate the middle of their symposium; what they'll get is increased awareness of how they work, push back against sloppy and incomplete thinking, and the modeling of effective approaches. It's not what they asked for (because they wouldn't have known how to ask for it), but it is what they needed.

# IMPACT

That's why I screwed up my courage to upset my client's plans and sidetrack the runaway train of their timeline. I shared with them the idea of a beginning, middle, and end, and the importance of honoring all three phases of their session. Fortunately for all of us, my concerns resonated.

Together we re-wrote their agenda giving adequate time and energy to each phase. The result was a better symposium, and some new insight on their part about how to construct an effective process. The Unit of Work was the simple model I used to help illuminate a better path forward.

# Chapter 12

# Noticing Energy Flow

As I covered in previous chapters, the goal of the Gestalt practitioner is to raise awareness as a way to mobilize the energy for change. So while we're noticing the present and raising awareness of the "here and now," we're doing it in service of building and sustaining energy.

Energy can be difficult to observe directly, but there are many clues one can perceive about when energy is high and when it is not. Take a step back from the details of any conversation, and you may notice the ebbs and flows of energy between and among individuals.

You might observe that some discussions feel like a raging stream full of rocks and rapids, loud and cacophonous, with people speaking quickly and forcefully, leaning forward or even rising out of their chairs to use vivid language and make emphatic points. The mood may be joyful, kinetic, or tense. The group may be zooming together towards its shared goals or splitting forcefully into eddies, back channels, and side issues.

Other conversations are more sedate, like a placid, lazy river. The tempo is low, with ideas inching slowly along. There may be moments of quiet as participants choose their words or reflect. The tone may be hushed or halting. Instead of leaning into the discussion, you might notice people speaking softly, leaning back, perhaps with their eyes closed. Some may be glancing at papers or a phone, or gazing into the distance.

Gestalt practitioners notice this kind of data to get insight into the energy that's present, and where and how it is moving – as a way to understand more about the moment. We pay attention to what holds people's interest and excitement, what generates energy, and what depletes it.

Most people completely ignore this data. They may experience the rise and fall of energy on some level, but those changes never register in their awareness. In Gestalt, we try to resist this pattern because we know intuitively that without energy very little can get done. Disconnect the power in an office building and the lights go off, the computers go down, and the cell phones stop charging. Eventually, those batteries will drain too, and productive work will grind to a halt.

In human dynamics, low energy can lead to low productivity and signal deeper problems. When people get stuck or distracted, it's often because they have lost the energy they need at key moments to accomplish their goals.

Too much energy can also be problematic. A wired individual may be productive working alone, but their frenzied activity can overwhelm and repel colleagues, spark conflict, and lead to hasty errors. High energy groups can feel thrilling, but the clamor can also be a barrier for talented people with a lower tolerance for chaos. And in the long haul, the momentum of a frenetic group is impossible to maintain. Eventually, people burn out.

# IMPACT

Maintaining the optimal amount of energy is a constant challenge. Some groups start off their projects with a bolt of enthusiasm and motivation, but then get bogged down and stuck. Others have difficulty just getting started, continually delaying initiatives that they know are essential. And some people get all the way to the brink of conclusion, but then cannot wrap things up cleanly and clearly.

To try to explain what's going on beneath the surface, Gestalt practitioners use a descriptive model called the Cycle of Experience to note those ebbs and flows of energy, and to look for places where it may be blocked or diverted. When people are effectively engaged, they maintain appropriate levels of energy through all six distinct phases: Sensation, awareness, mobilization, action, closure, and withdrawal.

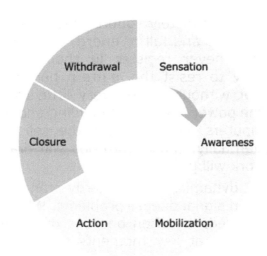

Consider an example of the Cycle in action: You are sitting in your favorite comfy chair, eyes closed, mind quiet, peacefully at rest. At some point, a buzzing sound enters your ears, but you remain unaware. After a few moments, your conscious mind notices the sound and makes meaning of it. You think, "Hm. I think I hear a mosquito. If it bites me, it will leave an itchy welt." Considering this unpleasant prospect breaks you out of your slumber, and you decide to swat the insect.

You open your eyes and look around, tuning your ears to narrow down the location of the buzzing. Your eyes focus on the motion of a black bug, and the tiny hairs on your arm bristle as you feel it land on your skin. You are now in action mode as you cock your hand to squash the attacker. Whack!

As you pull back your hand, you find a flattened mosquito on your arm, but no sign of your blood – so it seems that you got the mosquito before she got you. You drop the tiny corpse in the trash and forget about it. You go back to your chair, close your eyes again, and resume your restful moment.

| The Cycle of Experience | Example |
| --- | --- |
| **Sensation**: Taking in data about the environment through our senses | A buzzing sound enters your ears, and your skin feels a disturbance |
| **Awareness**: Noticing data that deserve attention, and beginning to make meaning | *"I think a mosquito is flying around me, and it will itch if it bites me."* |
| **Mobilization**: Overcoming inertia or distraction to focus on a mission | You decide to swat the insect |
| **Action**: Attempting to complete the mission | You hunt the mosquito and squash it with your hand |
| **Closure**: Acknowledging that the mission is complete | You drop the dead insect in the trash, and see if you were bitten |
| **Withdrawal**: Removing focus from the mission | You lose interest in the insect and close your eyes again |

It's easy to imagine key points in this Human v. Mosquito cycle when energy might have been blocked and the story might have worked out differently:

- Blocked sensation: You are wearing earplugs, so you never hear the mosquito in the first place. The mosquito bites you repeatedly. When you finally wake up, try to find the calamine lotion.

- Blocked awareness: You have fallen deeply asleep in your chair; the buzzing noise enters your ears, but because you're dozing you never become aware of it. Again, the mosquito feasts. (Salt can also take out some of the itch, BTW)

- Blocked mobilization: The buzzing sound wakes you up and you know a mosquito is nearby, but you are so tired you keep dozing anyway. More bites and welts.

- Blocked action: The sound of the mosquito rouses you from your rest, but before you begin the hunt you get distracted by a hilarious cat video on your phone. By the time the video finishes, the mosquito has done her deed and flown away.

- Blocked closure: You slap at the mosquito but never find its corpse...so you keep hunting for it, unsure who got whom. The adventure continues!

- Blocked withdrawal: The anxiety about being bitten turns into a kind of obsession; you focus your attention on tracking down buzzing sounds and killing mosquitos all over the building. Let's see how many you can bag.

At this point you might notice similarity to two other models I described in earlier chapters – The Ladder of Inference and the Unit of Work. With a little tinkering, you could overlay these three models together, since they are slightly different takes on many of the same dynamics.

# IMPACT

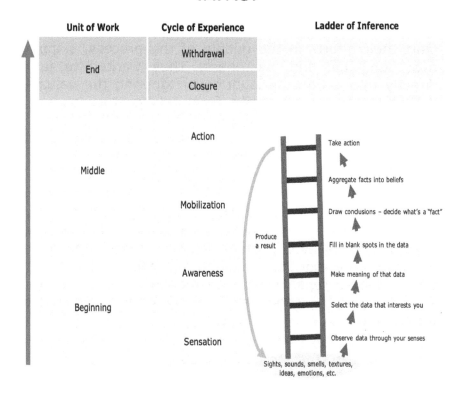

The Ladder of Inference from Chapter 6 describes the beginning and middle of the Cycle of Experience process -- sensation, awareness, mobilization, and action. The Ladder doesn't speak to the end of the process – which is closure and withdrawal.

A Cycle of Experience (as in the mosquito examples above) might be completed in a few seconds, and when a cycle is that brief we tend to have little difficulty mobilizing and maintaining our energy throughout. But in our professional lives some Units of Work last for months or years. Enormous projects, like the building of a cathedral, can take more than a century. (And complex endeavors like corporate mergers can *seem* to go on for generations.) When timeframes get stretched beyond our immediate attention, the energy we muster for doing the work will ebb and flow repeatedly. It's one reason big projects can start with a burst and then peter off into incompletion.

I've already described impatient clients who wanted to start their efforts in the middle of the process, skipping over sensation and awareness. They wanted to jump directly into action, discounting or ignoring the valuable data that they could derive from taking stock of who's present; acknowledging powerful emotions in the room like fear, anger, hopefulness, or pride; learning about stakeholders' needs and expectations; noticing how the physical environment might support or distract from the work; and more.

It's as if they heard a buzzing sound and decided to start slapping at their arms without ever determining whether mosquitos were even present. Maybe it's not a mosquito, but the refrigerator that's making that noise, in which case they'd need a repair technician more than a fly swatter. They jumped to action before really knowing what they were doing.

On the other side of the spectrum, groups and individuals can start strong but then stall out at a particular phase of the Cycle. It's as if there is a roadblock that keeps them from moving freely around the cycle and catches them each time they try. Despite their best efforts, they keep getting stuck.

Example: I once worked with a team of IT specialists for a government agency that had taken years to launch desperately-needed system upgrades. The project had been approved and the funding was in hand, but the assembled experts repeatedly delayed implementation so they could run more tests and consider more options.

While their superiors were extremely eager to see results, this team prided themselves in being careful and methodical. But their diligence ignored the desperate needs of the organization and the demands of their bosses. The group was unwilling or unable to move past sensation and awareness into action, and it ultimately made them ineffective.

Similarly, I worked with a media professional in an advocacy organization who was tasked to develop a set of simple audience metrics to track the group's social media growth. She had years of experience and obvious expertise, but could never get the project started, continually coming back to her supervisor for more clarification and information about what was needed. Like the government IT experts, she was stuck in awareness and unable to move into action. Months went by without her proposing any metrics; eventually, her inertia cost her that job.

While group meetings have different dynamics, the same patterns can emerge. I am often hired to facilitate strategic planning sessions, which can be high-energy meetings where participants get excited speculating about all the new projects they're going to tackle in the coming year. But plans that seem exciting at the retreat often lose their luster once people return to the office, where the energy for change can be depleted by the tedium of responding to all those emails that piled up while they were away.

In facilitator lingo, this is called "the Chandelier Effect," the common pattern of making grand plans under the hotel ballroom chandeliers, and then forgetting about those plans as soon as the meeting is over. Gestalt practitioners see this as something else: A group that has gotten stuck between mobilization and action.

I also work with organizations that can never bring anything to a close. Projects start with great enthusiasm, they make progress, and then they slow down without ever really ending. Such "zombie programs" can linger for years, long after they have outlived their usefulness. In fact, I used to have a car like that: When I'd put it in park and turn off the ignition, the engine would sputter and stop, and then after a momentary chugging noise, it would fire right back up again. Clearly, I needed a qualified Gestalt mechanic.

When groups are functioning well, they collect data, make meaning, mobilize their energy, take action, complete their tasks, and then move on to the next thing. One of my earliest clients is an excellent example of how to methodically move through all the stages of the Cycle of

Experience. The Outdoor Gear Exchange, a small retail business based in Burlington, Vermont used their initial retreats with me to take stock of opportunities and threats in their sector, and they laid out ambitious but actionable plans for growth and organizational change.

The staff and leaders left our early sessions feeling energized, and over the months and years that followed they harnessed their energy to implement nearly every strategy they had devised together. In doing so, they transformed their "mom and pop" operation into a multi-million dollar retail outlet with both a booming online market and successful bricks-and-mortar stores.

Habitually getting stuck in any one spot in the cycle is debilitating. People get exasperated when the pattern of "nothing gets finished" or "we can't get started" becomes obvious...and for the consultant that's another clue that there may be a systemic blockage in the group's Cycle of Experience. Those complaints are valuable data that something is happening.

Even short-term blockages in the Cycle can suck the energy from a room. I recently attended a large and raucous birthday dinner for a friend at a local restaurant. Our group was loud and boisterous during the meal, and everyone seemed to be having a great time. But then after the plates were cleared, the staff mysteriously disappeared. We waited and waited and waited. Was anyone going to bring us the check?

A typical restaurant meal has its own Cycle of experience, from taking in the scene at arrival (sensation and awareness), ordering and eating (mobilization and action), and then finally paying the bill and leaving (closure and withdrawal). For our birthday dinner, the Cycle got stuck at closure – and the energy of our group dropped like a lead weight.

For a consultant or leader, noticing such ebbs and flows of energy holds a wealth of valuable insight, but to gather that data one has to lean on the "foot outside the group," disconnecting slightly from the details of what's going on.

The trick is to pay attention to what people are doing and saying, but not too much.

The Gestalt practitioner looks for patterns that might correlate with energy. Moments of transition often hold clues. What happened before or after a change in tone or direction? You might observe things like

- The volume of a conversation increases or decreases

- Vivid language (e.g., the use of shocking words, provocative ideas, or strongly expressed emotions)

- Bland language (which tends to stupefy, and therefore distract)

- People rapidly interjecting and interrupting, or long pauses between comments

- Topics that generate jokes, conflicts, side conversations, or distracting tangents

- Your own feelings of interest, engagement, emotional connection, or boredom

Using the Cycle of Experience as a model, I might notice numerous blockages in an organization. I might observe issues and challenges that linger and recur without ever being resolved. I often hear clients complain that a problem "has been around forever" or that "we can't seem to move on," which suggests that the group is unable to progress with intention around its own Cycle of Experience.

I might also notice that some crises are dismissed or devalued by leaders, even though they could have serious implications. And I'm likely to see that the contributions of some (e.g., people perceived to have higher status) generate action, while others (e.g., people perceived to have lower status) do not.

Once I start noticing these patterns or sequences of events, a new level of curiosity can emerge. For example:

- "I wonder what it meant...when Casey mentioned the strategic plan, and it got very quiet in the room."

- "I wonder what it means that...every time we discuss the budget, people start yelling and cutting each other off."

- "I wonder what it meant that...someone made an awkward joke during JD's speech."

- "I wonder what it means that...they can't bring this topic to a satisfying conclusion."

In some cases, noticing these patterns can yield crucial hypotheses about blockages of energy. When Casey mentioned the strategic plan (in the first example above), maybe it became suddenly quiet because the group is holding some painful or awkward perception about the plan, or about how it's being implemented, or about Casey, or about something else. My task is to notice this disjunction and sharpen my curiosity about what that change in energy might be about. Is this an isolated incident? Does it always happen when the strategic plan is mentioned? Does it always happen when Casey speaks? Did Casey say something in particular that triggered the reaction?

In other cases, noticing these patterns can yield...nothing useful. Sometimes a change in energy is just a change in energy. Maybe the group is hungry, or tired, or hot, or cold, or bored and ready to move on to the next topic. Maybe you've misread the signals.

My role isn't to run every hypothesis to ground, but to be curious, open, and patient. Some questions won't get answered. Some hypotheses that seem exciting won't end up being right. And some changes in energy I observe won't, in the end, turn out to be significant.

Just recently I was facilitating a senior executive team for an international aid organization. After the first of two days together, several people lamented that "we never talk about the important issues," and "we're only scratching the surface."

Then at one point, the tone suddenly changed: Several participants became animated, speaking more quickly and interrupting one another. Instead of talking about the idea of talking about the issues, they started getting real: They were putting their true feelings out in the open and taking some risks.

Then the president of the company spoke up. He told a story about the organization's founding almost 70 years earlier, and about the reasons the Board had made some key decisions early in his tenure. As he talked, I looked around the room and noticed that the people who had been animated seconds earlier were now subdued. Many people looked down or looked at their hands. Some people gazed upwards. One person started to write a note.

What did this mean? By telling his story, the president had shifted the group's attention from the emotions and experiences articulated by the people in the room to focus on people who have been dead for decades. He had drained the energy of the moment by refocusing attention on people who were not present, and the actions they took in the past.

So I intervened, noting that the group has a habit of disempowering itself, as we had just witnessed. I called attention the rising energy I observed moments earlier, and how individuals squelched that progress by shifting their attention from the "here and now" to people who aren't present, and to actions that were taken so long ago. I quickly sketched the Cycle of Experience on a flip chart, and suggested that they could never get to energy and action because they kept spinning around in sensation and awareness.

As I finished my comments, I looked around to room to take in their reactions. Several people were nodding in affirmation, and a few had wry smiles on their faces. Even the president was now looking down and smiling to himself in a way that acknowledged the truth of the situation. I invited people to voice their reflections. "Yes," said the COO. "We do that all the time. We're doing it right now."

From that point forward, armed with a new frame of reference, the group policed itself, noticing its patterns and self-correcting. The ensuing conversation got much deeper, and important issues were voiced for the first time.

# IMPACT

It was a pivotal moment, when a small spark of insight about something that had been present for years suddenly grew into a flash of new awareness. With their eyes now opened, the team mobilized its energy to change the way they behaved, and put new focus on taking action.

# Chapter 13
# Pain, Resistance, and Impact

I rarely get asked by prospective clients to come in and "keep things the same." A typical client usually hires me to help their people and processes get better, faster, easier, more efficient, more effective, broader, deeper, smarter, and/or more connected. They want me to help them reap the benefits of change.

But change, by its nature, exacts costs that are borne and tolerated unevenly. Some costs are easy to quantify and tend to get a lot of attention – things like financial costs, lost time and productivity, and squandered opportunities. Other costs typically get overlooked because they are difficult to quantify and therefore easy to discount: Confusion, anxiety, fear, grief, loss, anger, stress, etc.

# IMPACT

As costs bubble to the surface they become more apparent and personal, and even the most enthusiastic change-advocate may look for ways to off-load the burdens onto others. If that doesn't work, they may try to slow or redirect the process, even if it's an initiative that they themselves had previously championed.

Such inconsistency and second thoughts don't mean that these people are crazy: It just means they're human. We are all wired to resist change at the same time we crave it, pushing ahead while simultaneously holding back as a way to protect ourselves from unpleasant, unwanted, or unpredictable situations. We want things to be better and different, but we're reluctant to pay the price.

This runs directly counter to many of the narratives we may tell about ourselves as decisive leaders. Case in point: I see myself as a person who makes a decision and sticks to it, moving forthrightly from Point A to Point B. But if I pull back and look at the bigger picture, I have to acknowledge that I actually spend a fair amount of time zigzagging about, and then afterwards I create a post-hoc story about my clarity of mind and direction that puts all that dithering in the best possible light.

While I may aspire to be a courageous disrupter, I simultaneously promote and resist change in myself and my environment. It's a common pattern. The same ambivalent push-pull emerges for people whether they're initiating a change themselves (e.g., deciding to quit your job and start your own business) or have change imposed from the outside, as in a corporate restructuring.

Organizational consultant William Bridges mapped some of the ways resistance shows up in people experiencing change from any such source. His transition model acknowledges that change swaps-out our feelings of comfort for painful emotions like denial, anxiety, and confusion – unpleasant experiences that naturally generate self-protective push-back inside us. Over time, we may reorient to the new situation and embrace our opportunities, but early in the process we are more likely to notice the pain, be less productive, and feel more resistant.

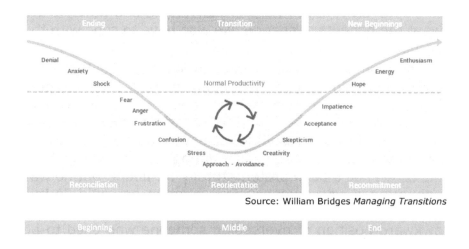

Source: William Bridges *Managing Transitions*

You might notice that the Bridges model also has a distinct beginning, middle, and end (which I've highlighted with a separate row at the bottom of the graphic). Bridges maps neatly against some of the Gestalt theories I've already discussed, even though he switches his perspective a bit. He puts the ending first, meaning the ending of the status quo, and he puts the beginning last, to highlight the beginning of the new paradigm. And yes, this also looks a lot like Lewin's Unfreeze-Change-Re-freeze model that I mentioned in Chapter 11.

I've shared the Bridges approach with people I know who are in the throes of a difficult professional or personal transition, and most have found its ideas to be comforting. Change hurts, so when they've found themselves pulling back during a volatile moment, turning away, or having second thoughts about a promotion or move to another city, it's not necessarily a sign of weakness, dysfunction, or poor decision-making on their part. It's simply a typical part of the process. It feels bad because it's supposed to feel bad...and that realization takes some of the sting out of the situation.

Let's stay with that beginning phase of the change process – when disorientation, disruption, and resistance are high – because frankly that's the part everyone wants to skip over. And I'm here to deliver the bad news: If we want the benefits of change, we also have to cope with the costs.

For example: One acquaintance of mine recently took a surprisingly big leap up his organizational ladder, jumping several rungs to become the boss of his immediate supervisor. (Yes, he's kind of a star.) While his new responsibilities and resulting raise were thrilling, the whole situation was also deeply disorienting for him. Throughout his career, he'd been preternaturally confident, but he was now gripped with anxiety about whether he could do this new job, and irritated that his superiors had put him in the awkward position of overseeing someone who used to be his boss. He spent the first few months in a low-level panic that he'd flop spectacularly, his incompetence would be discovered, and his promotion would be reversed.

Rather than acknowledge these feelings, he took a stoic approach. He kept his concerns to himself and buckled down. He worked longer and longer hours, hoping to substitute quantity for quality. The strategy worked: He was able to keep his new job and became more comfortable in his role, but at the high cost of allowing his health to fall into disarray.

The same happens on an organizational level. I can't count the number of clients who come to me hoping to implement some sort of change while avoiding dissent and minimizing pushback, getting directly to a magical state of "buy in" by taking a short-cut through all the uncomfortable bits. Those leaders want happy employees and the benefits of change without accepting or adapting to any of its costs.

This is when I have to cautiously deliver a reality check: Change always produces pain, even if you don't (or don't want to) see it. That pain can be personal, physical, psychic, emotional, or all of the above. It can be quick to arrive and depart, or it may linger, and it can come in widely varying degrees of intensity, scope, and survivability.

People at the top of the system tend to find ways to avoid pain by sloughing it off to the people below. Middle managers often bear the brunt of implementing reorganization plans, sometimes by inflicting costs on others (e.g., by laying-off or reassigning subordinates), or they may take the layoff bullet themselves. And it's at the bottom of the corporate pyramid where the long-term pains of disruption and restructurings tend to pile up.

For the Gestaltist, there are a few takeaways: Change creates pain, and pain produces resistance. Change and pain – and therefore resistance – tend to be proportional to one another. Big change tends to produce big pain, which in turn produces big resistance. And resistance – an active or passive pushing back against a perceived threat – takes and consumes energy. That, in turn, affects the amount of energy available to do everything else.

Because of all the pain involved (and even the anticipation of possible pain), resistance is to be expected in every situation when change is on the table. Wishing resistance away will not make it so, and we shouldn't even try.

We accept the idea of pain in the human body as a natural and beneficial response to injury: The *ouch*! we feel when we slice our finger with a kitchen knife teaches us that knives are sharp and dangerous, and that cutting your finger with a knife is a bad idea. The pain feels awful, and its awfulness is instructive.

Similarly, resistance is a healthy, positive, and natural balancing force that signals the presence of anxiety or risk. In organizational settings, resistance allows people the time and space to make meaning of new and fraught circumstances, give voice to concerns, manage discomfort, adjust, and find ways to survive.

So for leaders and consultants, the goal isn't to deny or avoid resistance. It can't be done! The goal is to anticipate and manage it.

# IMPACT

An excess of resistance, like an excess of bodily pain, can become overwhelming all by itself. It can push everything else aside, leaving a group or individual stuck, de-energized, and immobilized. When resistance is unmanaged, it can become the mortal enemy of productive change, sapping or blocking the energy needed to make progress.

We can't look inside other people to see their pain, but we can notice the ways pain and resistance color their behavior. Effective Gestalt practitioners are always on the lookout for those signs and signals. Like the apocryphal Inuit people who allegedly have fifty different words for varieties of snow, Gestaltists have become resistance connoisseurs, parsing and labeling all the different permutations of self-protective behavior that typically show up in ourselves, our clients, and their organizations. Resistance behaviors can be clumped into seven groups:

 When an environment becomes intolerable, unsafe, or stressful, some people simply shut down as an act of self-preservation. Such **desensitization** is common in unpleasant or unrewarding workplaces, or in times of destabilizing change.

Case in point: When the news of the world feels unrelentingly negative, I stop reading The New York Times: I cope by blocking out the offending stimulus, like an ostrich sticking my head in the sand. When I see clients overwhelmed by problems or frozen by too many options, I roll out the business aphorisms: "We don't have to boil the ocean." "You don't have to eat the elephant in one bite."

People who are desensitizing might exhibit a flat affect. They might stare at their phone, or defer topics saying, "Let's talk about this later," or, "It doesn't matter to me." They might try to shift focus or disparage a critical issue as irrelevant, boring, or too sensitive.

**Projection**: Another way people may cope with feelings of powerlessness is to insist that they alone understand the perceptions, beliefs, opinions, or attitudes of their colleagues. They may repackage their own views as being held by others, saying things like, "You're clearly upset," or "I know you support that!" – when in fact, they have no idea. Or they might make grand statements like, "Everyone knows the right way to go here."

Projection can offer a safe way for people to express anxieties without having to personally own them. But projected views can be confusing, bogging a conversation down with unsupported claims and counter-claims.

And things can get hot. People resent being told by others how they think and feel, so this form of resistance can also produce some nasty backlash from peers.

**Introjection** is pretty easy to spot. When you hear definitive statements with the words "should," "must," or "need to," or absolute declarations about what can and cannot be done, the speaker is surrendering authority and insisting others do the same. You might imagine such people having swallowed whole a set of restrictions and certainties that, once fully ingested, are now entirely impervious to discussion.

Such people cite rules, limits, or unshakeable expectations, or insist on irrefutable norms that must be accepted; doing so can allow them to embrace a comforting story in a stressful situation, throwing responsibility and pain onto others.

But introjections can sit like a fog, causing confusion and fatigue as you disentangle what is true from what is merely asserted. In the extreme, demagogues can use introjection to blame others and mobilize righteous indignation rather than productive action.

Some people may find their voice continually blocked by an unseen inner obstacle, a form of resistance known as **retroflection**. You might observe a person stop themselves suddenly in a conversation mid-sentence, or hear their words trail off to inaudible mumbles.

You may hear critical self-talk like, "I shouldn't have said that," or "What am I doing here?" Or there may be seemingly compulsive behaviors like biting one's fingernails, scratching one's arms, or constantly rearranging in one's seat.

Retroflection is a coping mechanism against a hostile environment, but it blocks personal connections with peers. Retroflection silences a person's voice, which reduces the group's ability to communicate and collaborate.

One of the most seductive forms of resistance doesn't feel like resistance at all; it tends to feel great! But when you observe groups or individuals who always agree, never contradict one another or argue, and who portray themselves more as family than co-workers, you may be observing **confluence**. In such cases, people may go to excessive lengths to align their views and submerge differences, to set aside or stifle dissent, and maintain a jolly feeling of bonhomie. Listen for boasts like, "We always agree!" and lots of gentle ribbing and joking. The camaraderie can be seductive.

We humans are wired to form tribes, so this is understandable. We are constantly seeking alignment and conformity with others; "going along to get along" scratches a deep primordial itch.

But groups need productive conflict and honesty to illuminate differences of opinion and values, and benefit fully from each person's experience and intuition. Author Patrick Lencioni identifies such disagreements as an essential and irreplaceable characteristic of successful teams. And repeated studies have shown that diversity and divergent views help eliminate misperceptions and stimulate creativity.

If you scratch below the surface of a giddy, happy, unified team, you'll almost always find stifled disagreements and roiling irritation. When confluence takes hold, people hold back their contrary views and submerge their own dissents. This in turn lowers energy (especially for those with less power and privilege), increases complacency (especially among those with more power and privilege), and fosters cynicism.

 At times, we all seek ways to avoid discomfort by shifting attention from something important to something trivial. Such **deflections** can come in the form of enjoyable diversions, like jokes or humorous asides that lighten a dark mood or provide relief from an awkward topic. Deflection also comes in the form of shocking language that draws attention to itself – or conversely as vague, abstract, or indirect language that lulls people into a stupefying fog, like an octopus hiding behind a disorienting cloud of ink.

Deflections can be a welcome release at a tense moment, a kind of "sugar that makes the medicine go down." But when over-used, deflection can block attention to what really matters, giving interactions an inappropriately superficial or unserious tone.

And worse: People with power and privilege can use deflection to divert attention from the needs of others. For instance, I've seen men make inappropriate jokes when women raise issues around gender in the workplace. And I've heard white people draw attention to themselves when confronted around issues of race. Such deflections reinforce existing power imbalances and suppress needed conversation.

# IMPACT

Each of us needs a healthy ego to separate ourselves as individuals from others, and to create a unique and  compelling presence. But too much self-regard can become **egotism**, in which a person focuses excessively on self and pushes back against help from others. Statements like, "I'm ok!," or "That doesn't apply to me" can be seen as signs of independence and courage, but they can also signal an unwillingness to learn, connect with others, or see new perspectives. At worst, such behavior can slip into excessive self-regard and narcissism, and may be resented as a lack of empathy or for "acting as if the rules don't apply."

All of these forms of resistance are normal, typical, and not a sign of dysfunction for individuals and groups (at least to some degree). In fact, we humans are champion resisters! It's likely that each of us has engaged in every flavor of resistance at one time or another...and might employ several strategies at once!

Most of us have our own special favorite forms of resistance, our "go to" ways to manage pressure, stress, and anxiety. These behaviors may be most obvious in moments of change. The world can be a scary place, so resistance is simply part of how we get through a given day.

It's how I get through my day. I often procrastinate – which is a kind of deflection. I typically defer unpleasant tasks (like paying bills or unloading the dishwasher) by distracting myself with relatively easy and enjoyable time-killers; it's only after I run out of text messages, crossword puzzles, and pointless web scrolling that I eventually get down to business. And when talking with friends I often crack jokes and tell anecdotes, which is another form of deflection from the important conversations and meaningful connections that might otherwise take place.

# IMPACT

I'm also prone to resisting through egotism, acting as if I don't really need the help or wisdom of others. I typically avoid taking professional development classes, and when I take a class, I tend to distance myself from the faculty or gently question their expertise (at least to myself).

When reading the scholarly work of colleagues in my field, I quickly find myself feeling bored, distracted, and eager to do something else. When friends offer assistance, I usually tell them I've got things under control (whether I do or not). Recently, a close friend stared me dead in the eyes and made this sharp and startling indictment: "You never ask for help!" He was exasperated, and it wasn't a compliment. Thanks, friend. Message received.

Even though it may be counterproductive, my expressions of egotism maintain my sense of self by pushing others and their insights away, and reasserting my internal narrative that I am wise and self-sufficient. It's something I'm still working on.

In my family life, I have tended to seek confluence, sanding down the edges of conflict and overlooking perceived slights to maintain a high level of comity and connectedness. As a result, important issues with my mother, brother, and in-laws have gone years without ever being addressed!

In awkward social situations, I desensitize. Listening to someone make objectionable political comments at a dinner party, I'll probably look away, take a sip of my drink, or poke at the food on my plate. I'm reluctant to confront the outrageous substance of what's being said, so I'll just disconnect from the conversation and hope the topic passes. If that doesn't work, I'll try to deflect by making a joke or changing the subject.

I'm less likely to use introjection, projection, or retroflection in my daily life. These aren't my preferred forms of resistance, but I definitely see them in others. My ex-husband often projects, asserting that he has clear insight into why someone has said or done something important, even though he can't point to any evidence beyond his own certainty.

I have a dear friend who often introjects, framing his life choices around what he *should* be doing by this point in his career, or what *has to* be accomplished. And I often think of a brilliant colleague who stifles her best ideas mid-sentence with self-critiques like, "I shouldn't be saying this," or "I don't know what I'm talking about," before trailing off into silence.

## Creating impact

When you tune your antenna to resistance, you start seeing it everywhere. The goal of the Gestalt practitioner isn't to stamp out resistance (since that would be impossible), but to notice it, acknowledge it, and manage it with intention.

If you're not seeing resistance, you're probably looking in the wrong places. And if you're looking in the wrong places it may be because, like me, you tend to get brought into a project by a boss who's also looking for resistance in the wrong places.

Bosses see the world from their own privileged vantage point, and they tend to interact primarily with people who are similar and hold similar views. These leaders don't realize how much pain and resistance exists because, in part, they don't know what they're looking for.

Others don't see the pain because they don't want to know – and they really don't want to deal with it. A few organizational leaders I've worked with over the years have all but admitted that they view the resistance of their colleagues as a pest or a cancer that must be crushed, silenced, or shoved to the side.

I've learned that at the beginning of a new project, I won't hear too much from the lower reaches of the org chart, even when I start poking. People without power generally have few ways to express their opposition or get their complaints noticed. Line workers adapt by disguising their dissent, laying low to avoid retribution.

And not everyone in an organization will hold the same interests and information at any given moment, so the pain might be very different from person to person. Some will quickly rally to the need to champion a proposed change and may be willing to take on more discomfort for a greater good. Others who feel perfectly content with the status quo will look at change initiatives with far more skepticism. As a result, they'll resent the resulting pain more acutely.

You can generally perceive more resistance the further you wander from the levers of power. And when people feel that change is being imposed without their consultation, the intensity of their resistance can ratchet even higher.

Turning a blind eye to resistance is a sure recipe for disaster. In recent years, I worked with a company that was intent on boosting productivity and broadening its revenue base, so the Chief Operating Officer envisioned a sweeping reorganization to regain their edge. With little consultation beyond his immediate colleagues, he created a plan that realigned key revenue-producing parts of the company, re-wrote job descriptions and lines of authority, adopted new metrics for success, overhauled employees' compensation scheme, and even required veteran employees to reapply for their jobs.

The president and the leadership team quickly endorsed the plan. They were excited about the innovative approaches, the cutting-edge matrix management model, and all the new synergies that would result. The case was compelling, so they were certain their employees would readily jump on board. They called a company-wide meeting to explain the reorganization, presenting it as a completed final package.

The response was not as hoped. Long-time staff reacted with shock, dismay, and feelings of betrayal. They asked tough questions, proposed amendments, and challenged the very premise of the reorg. But since leaders had sold this as a done deal, there was no way to constructively channel any of the pushback or mollify the strong emotions. The new plan was implemented as originally presented.

# IMPACT

Resistance quickly mushroomed everywhere. The mood in the office soured, and tensions ran high. People started taking mental health days to manage their stress. They updated their resumes and began looking for new jobs. Many left, leaving those who remained to pick up the slack. Suddenly understaffed, the company missed internal deadlines, and revenue dropped rather than increasing. The new plan backfired, and it took many months to realize that the outcomes would not get better.

Ultimately the reorganization was shelved and the COO resigned, but by then the damage had already been done. Years later, and after multiple leadership changes, the after-effects can still be felt.

This reorganization failed for the same reason many strategic plans and systems changes crash on the rocks, partially implemented or worse: The leaders overlooked the pain their plans would cause, and never had a strategy for managing the myriad forms of resistance that ensued.

There is a better way: Gestalt practitioners know to anticipate and welcome resistance, to view it as normal and constructive, and to build resistance management into any program or initiative. By inviting pain and resistance into the open, we enable our clients and colleagues to identify and address submerged risks, accommodate the needs of employees, and increase the chances that real change can take place.

Consider the social change slogan, "Nothing about us without us." To minimize resistance, the people who do the work must have a say in how the work is done.

And when you do, there's a bonus: You get access to a treasure trove of new ideas that can be implemented without a lot of employee pushback. A colleague of mine worked with an urban medical center where nurses were constantly buffeted with new procedures and policies dreamed up by hospital administrators aiming to reduce costs and increase efficiency. In the nurses' minds, each wave of "innovation" was worse than the ones that preceded it, making it harder for them to do their jobs and care for patients. They adapted grudgingly to each new policy as it was implemented, but eventually found workarounds and short-cuts that made their jobs easier while subverting the intent of their superiors.

After years of hardening resistance, my colleague took the radical step of inviting the nurses to propose ways to make their workplace more efficient. Finally invited to the table as peers, they suggested simple improvements that aligned with the realities of their daily work, and after some skepticism the hospital allowed their most promising ideas to take effect. The result was a happier staff, higher compliance with the new operating procedures, and (yes) more efficiency and lower costs.

The downside of getting such buy-in is that it requires time and energy, and many of us are too impatient for that kind of investment. Executives are in a rush to begin right away, end right away, and not waste a moment to think about what is being done. They are anxious to leap before they look, and let the consequences be damned.

Some organizations can get away with such high-handed tactics. They can pound the ill-fitting puzzle pieces (e.g., their employees) hard enough to jam them into the new organizational design because the leaders are largely impervious to the discomforts and resistance of others. Thankfully, this is not a world in which most of us live.

Reorganizations, mergers, strategic plans, and innovation programs all require enormous investments of time and energy to dream up new processes and systems, retrain employees, realign talent, and more. Heedlessly jumping ahead without incorporating the insights and needs of employees is almost always a poor financial choice. It's also exhausting and unsustainable.

Integrating rank-and-file employees at the start of the process is a big help in lowering the degree and intensity of pain, but no matter what you do you'll still see resistance in the everyday life of the organization. The Gestaltist must be prepared to not just identify resistance when it happens, but also to intervene effectively.

# IMPACT

Many of the most effective interventions can appear unremarkable. The simplest (and sometimes most impactful) response to resistance is to simply call attention to the behavior once you've observed it. When I hear a telltale phrase or see a concerning behavior, I start my comment with the words, "I notice that..." and then name the data without adding any interpretation or valuation.

I might say, "I notice we've started making jokes now rather than focusing on the issues we were discussing." Or, "I hear people saying things like, 'We should stick to this policy' but without citing any authority for the statement." Or, "I notice that the room suddenly became quiet."

If they hear my input, they can start to make new meaning of the current moment. And if that happens, they will have raised their awareness, and helped mobilize their energy for change. It's Gestalt 101.

This approach may seem odd to you. If so, you aren't alone. Such interventions can be both simple and effective, but their simplicity can also make them seem daunting. Is it really that easy to raise someone's awareness and mobilize their energy to move past a habitual form of resistance or embrace meaningful change in their organization? It actually is.

When I took the iGold course, I shared that skepticism. Each time my consulting team worked with real life clients I found myself asking, "Will this really work?"

In each case, we met with a client organization for about 90 minutes, after which we were instructed to devise a modest intervention we could implement in just a couple of hours the following afternoon. The clients knew we were experienced professionals. Although we were learning a new craft, they brought their real issues and expected real results.

We spent very little time with each client, and barely had time to offer much in the way of an intervention. Nevertheless, the organizations we supported were blown away by the results we could achieve. As practitioners, we were amazed too. We observed first-hand the powerful impacts of our modest efforts, but we still couldn't fully believe what we were seeing.

In South Africa, our consulting team worked with a small company in two brief interactions over two days, and at the end we received effusive feedback about what a difference our interventions had made. They told us they felt changed by the experience. We were gob-smacked.

After saying our good-byes, our team giddily piled back into the van for the return ride to our hotel. We could barely contain our excitement about how successful we had been, and the glowing feedback we had received. We reveled in our shared feelings of exhilaration and relief.

Then suddenly a member of our group interrupted with a perplexed look on her face. "Wait a minute, Paul!" she demanded. "Is that it?! Is that all we're supposed to do?!"

It turns out: That's it.

The lesson of that day has been reinforced for me many times since: The Gestalt practitioner can facilitate enormous change with a very modest intervention. For both the client and the consultant, the effects can be indescribable.

# IMPACT

# Part 3: The End

*"Now this is not the end.*
*It is not even the beginning of the end.*
*But it is, perhaps, the end of the beginning."*

Winston Churchill

# Chapter 15

# Impact and Resilience in Groups

The role of the intervener is to, well...intervene – to take a step forward and do (or not do) something in support of the client's needs. Gestalt practitioners intervene to raise awareness and mobilize energy for change. But what is intervention? For most of my career, I believed my job was to "do something" and to be noticed (preferably by a grateful client) for having done it.

That something could be to reframe a conversation so it could be more productive, make space for quieter participants to contribute, or hem in a chatty speaker who took the discussion off on an unproductive tangent. I also learned over time that keeping my mouth shut and staying out of the way could be a useful intervention too.

# IMPACT

What I came to see through Gestalt is that each of these interventions isn't a single act but rather the fluid realization of four distinct roles that I had previously rushed through without considering their complexity. The intervener plays all four parts, whether wittingly or not:

- Sensing: Gestaltists arrive ready to collect data with our five senses, our emotional receptors, and our sixth sense (intuition) open for inputs. We have our antennas up, our radar on, and our hearts open. We are in Receive Mode.

- Noticing (Awareness): We're paying attention to the data that comes in, giving it respect and credence. We are interested in whatever might happen, allowing ourselves to be surprised by unexpected inputs and the feelings, sensations, or ideas that result. Since we know we enter every process with our own biases and habits, we are also on the lookout for data we might typically overlook or devalue.

- Hypothesizing: We group, parse, and sift the data we've received, and ask ourselves, "What might this mean...if anything?" Because we always have incomplete information, we sit with the uncertainty of never really knowing for sure whether what we're perceiving is useful and actionable data, or just noise.

- Acting/Not Acting: Given what we have sensed, noticed, and hypothesized, we take an action intended to support the client's needs. Or, we withhold outward action and instead continue to be present, take in data, and revise our hypotheses as appropriate. As I've noted before, choosing to not act is also an intervention.

Yes, this looks a lot like the Cycle of Experience and the Ladder of Inference. All of these tools help me slow down and see complexity in something I had previously viewed in more naïve and simplistic terms.

Before my Gestalt training, I used to perform all four roles in an instant without much self-awareness. I'd hear something in a conversation, decide it was significant, decide what it meant, and then immediately say or do something in response. In many cases, my intervention seemed to form in my mouth as I was saying the words, without ever having spent any time beforehand in my conscious brain. It was as if I was hearing my idea for the very first time as I was speaking it.

Clearly this is a gift. I am very good at moving very fast.

But speed had costs. Sometimes I would react too quickly and based on too little data, so my hypothesis was faulty. Often I would interrupt something interesting that was developing, pushing my ideas to the forefront when the group was working on their own stuff.

Most troubling, I was doing work for the group instead of facilitating them doing the work for themselves. I was trying to make myself indispensable, intervening to fix problems...when my job as a facilitator was to empower them to fix their own problems.

The client's ability to fix their own problems is the basis of their resilience, and I now see that it's the long-term goal every consultant or leader should be working towards. When a group is fully empowered, they manage themselves effectively and don't need someone else telling them what to do and how to behave. Now I aim to facilitate sustainability rather than dependence.

Facilitators and servant leaders exist to serve the needs of others, to empower them to do their work, manage their boundaries, achieve their goals as effectively as possible, and otherwise get out of the way. Servant leaders intervene to remove obstacles, provide resources, direction and information from elsewhere in the organization, and offer compensation or evaluation.

Facilitating resilience is at the core of Gestalt. When I get hired by a client, they invite me in to provide something that's missing; sometimes it's a process, a set of insights, or a unique presence. My obligation is to help identify those missing elements, supply what can't be immediately resourced internally, and do it in a way that empowers them to take up the mantle of providing those elements on an ongoing basis without me. My goal is to ultimately make myself redundant and unnecessary. When I'm successful, they discover they can do it themselves.

This happened with the Outdoor Gear Exchange, the sporting goods client from Vermont that I cited in Chapter 12. In my initial work with the company, I helped them unravel some longstanding points of confusion, raised their awareness about gaps in their thinking, and showed them techniques for facilitating dialogue. And after about four of five years of hiring me for a series of projects, they figured out how to do all those things without me. As they developed their own skills and proficiencies, my work with them dried up. It's a sign of their growth and success.

Moving deliberately through the Four Roles of the Intervener, slowing down to take in more data, and realizing that I don't have to always be acting to be of value has helped broaden my range as a consultant. Sometimes I still match the impatient mode that my clients seem to prefer, operating with my "pedal to the metal," blurting out my interventions so quickly that I haven't even had time to think about them.

But I also love that I now have a new gear, and that I can thrive in circumstances where a slower approach is more effective. Because this more relaxed mode doesn't come naturally, I've had to develop two self-management techniques to break my own mental and behavioral patterns and help myself operate differently.

As I mentioned in Chapter 4, I coach myself to slow down by taking a small half-step backwards; once I do, my perspective shifts dramatically. Doing so reminds me to take in the entire room, all the people and the elements of the space, the things that are being said and those that are unsaid, the energy, and anything else that I might perceive by observing this moment in its totality. Stepping back pulls my attention away from the thing I'm bursting to say or do, at least for a moment. It reminds me that I can take in more data, and maybe intervene with a bit more context and finesse.

# IMPACT

In other situations, when I can feel the bubbling sensation in my chest that means I'm anxious to say or do something I'm convinced will be essential and smart and impactful...I stop myself to notice how important it has become for me to add my voice into what's happening in front of me.

Instead of moving fast as I so desperately want to, I close my mouth and count silently to thirty. While I'm counting, I wait to see whether whatever dynamic had me so excited is continuing, or whether the conversation has shifted. I'm waiting to see whether someone else in the room will say or do something to address what I saw going on.

Because I'm such an extravert and so eager to demonstrate my value, this holding back is particularly difficult for me...but I love the impact it can have. I've seen how hanging back can shift the energy in a conversation and open up new awareness for myself and my clients. I'm learning that I can be of value with my mouth closed and my eyes open. And I'm learning that voluntarily taking my voice out of the mix can serve as a tacit invitation to others in the group to step forward and take more responsibility for managing their boundaries and behaviors.

Another change in my practice is that my interventions themselves are less consistently directive than they used to be. Before my Gestalt training, I would typically notice something I didn't like, and immediately suggest a way to fix it. I might see people yawning or glancing at their watches, and quickly say, "Let's take a break!"

I now see that it's more effective to raise awareness than to give direction. Being less directive opens a space for others to be leaders themselves. In such moments, I can model productive attention to the "here and now," and invite the group to become more empowered and resilient.

It took me a while to figure out how to do any of this. Since I had unconsciously mashed together all Four Roles of the Intervener, I was also mashing together the products of each role – the data produced by sensing and awareness, hypotheses I might develop, and the intervention I might take. Now I try to operate with more intention and measure, picking and choosing which kind of interaction might work best, and then seeing what happens.

Now when I sense a shift in mood and notice people yawning or glancing at their watches, I might simply name the data and say, "I notice some people yawning or glancing at their watches," and see how others react. Or I might share a hypothesis like, "I wonder if people are feeling a bit tired right now," and see if anyone agrees. Or I could still be my old directive self, and instruct people with something like, "Let's take a break."

In some groups, naming the data might be all that's needed to spur someone to suggest some action on their own, perhaps to rally their focus and push through the work at hand. Simply raising awareness about what I observed (people in the room yawning or looking at their watches) might be enough to mobilize their energy to act. Each time participants successfully take the initiative, it makes it more likely they'll repeat that behavior after I'm gone.

In other groups, my citing of the data alone lands with a clunk. Instead of seeing it as a spur to take responsibility, my comments are met by silence and blank stares. Participants don't know how to react, so the interaction feels awkward and stilted.

Perhaps this group isn't used to hearing such unadorned observations, or they might need more guidance and modeling before they are able to mobilize their energy appropriately. It could also be that I haven't done a very good job of articulating the data in a way they can hear it. As a consultant, I never really know how such interventions will work out until I try them.

Fortunately, if one acts with intention and is able to stay engaged, even awkward moments have value. Wait long enough, and something will happen. And when it does, you can start the process all over by sensing that particular moment, making note of whatever has your attention, generating hypotheses, and considering your possible interventions.

# Chapter 16

# Impact and Resilience in Individuals

As I noted in Chapter 1, coaching and facilitation are closely related, but they are not quite identical. Coaches tend to work with individuals and very small groups; facilitators tend to work with larger groups, organizations, and coalitions. In each case, the practitioner seeks to raise awareness and mobilize energy to support impactful change.

But of course there's more to it. I've found that coaching projects look and feel different from facilitation projects. The "ask" at the beginning is different. In the middle, the focus of the work is different. And at the end, the outcome looks and feels different too.

Coaching and facilitation are clearly related to one another. Perhaps they are more like cousins than siblings.

# IMPACT

When I am approached by someone looking for a coach, they almost always start by describing a challenge they are facing. Perhaps they are struggling with the responsibilities of a new workplace or following a promotion. Often, people look to a coach when they feel stuck, blocked by an unproductive pattern, or confused about how to move forward in their career or personal life. Or an employer might provide a coach to an under-performing employee in hopes of fixing a troubling shortcoming or resolving a mismatch with the organizational culture.

My coaching clients tend to be engaged in some sort of struggle; sometimes they are in a moment of crisis. Only rarely do they describe their entry into the coaching relationship as a moment of opportunity.

Most facilitation and OD projects start differently. While the occasional facilitation gig starts with a plea to fix a problem too, like "Help us surmount internal silos that keep us apart" or "Help us repair trust issues," more facilitation gigs are framed around opportunities. Clients ask me to support more dialogue, encourage better understanding, develop greater transparency, facilitate agile decision-making, or hone a sharper focus on their shared mission.

Perhaps because the entry point is different, the exit point feels different too. My coaching projects rarely work towards a definitive end point; they simply conclude when the client says it's time to conclude. In contrast, facilitation projects are typically bounded by either time (e.g., a day-long offsite), the completion of a task (e.g., agreement on a new strategy), or some combination of both.

Because coaching projects typically bring together one coach and one coaching client, the tenor of the interaction tends to be more personal and intimate than in group work. When coaching an individual, I have sometimes mockingly been referred to as a "corporate therapist." I don't embrace this description, but I get it: The boundary between coaching and therapy can seem a bit blurry. Coaching and therapy can get into similar terrain because (regardless of the context) we all want the same things: To be seen, respected, and appreciated.

# IMPACT

And I caution my clients that even though the joke is amusing, I'm really, really, really not a therapist. I lack the training and skills to plumb as deeply as a therapist might, to diagnose illness, or prescribe medication. If they need therapy, they should hire a therapist.

Lots of people need the help a coach can offer. As I discussed in Chapter 5, the world is more volatile, uncertain, complex, and ambiguous than ever before, so each of us has to keep finding new ways to adapt to the rapid and destabilizing environment in which we operate. Just getting through the day can be a struggle!

And it's not just the outside world that is in turmoil. None of us is static and unchanging either. If we're lucky, we are growing and learning new things, and (hopefully) advancing towards more responsibility and authority. As our roles change, our expectations for ourselves change too...and so do the expectations placed on us by others.

I talk with many colleagues these days who acknowledge (especially after the onset of the COVID pandemic) feeling unsettled or adrift. Some have lost sight of their personal destination or are feeling overwhelmed. Others feel themselves pulled down by anxiety, loss, or disappointment.

Ironically, many report the most distress at moments when you might imagine them to experience new energy and enthusiasm – as they change jobs, move up, start a new business, or take on an ambitious project. It turns out that arriving at the brink of success can be enormously stressful all by itself.

In Chapter 13 I shared a story about one such acquaintance; his big promotion brought on a psychological burden that wore down his health. His new job reinforced his imposter syndrome, leaving him unsure why he got the promotion, or whether he truly deserved it. He began to doubt the skills, talents, and accomplishments that had brought him to that point, afraid that he would be exposed as a fraud.

# IMPACT

Another client told me she was ready to ditch her government career to fulfill her lifelong dream of becoming a full-time fiction writer. She had already written numerous stories she felt confident about...but she felt stuck at the threshold of her new career, unable to submit her work to prospective publishers.

Of course she feared rejection, but she was even more worried about the opposite reaction: Adoration. What would it mean if people loved her writing? Would they interrupt her in restaurants to ask for autographs? Would she have to leave her comfortable home for out-of-town book signings and conferences? Would her friends and family see her differently? She feared that either failure or success would upset her status quo, so she stayed locked in place for years while her dreams (and her manuscripts) gathered dust.

The prospect of a major transition can surface all sorts of anxiety about one's place in the newly emerging reality, and even ambitious people can find themselves suddenly stuck. To move forward, you might need an alternative narrative like this: The emotional turmoil I'm experiencing is typical and expected for a person in my situation. It's likely that today's pain and uncertainty will abate over time as I become more focused and effective in my new role.

This is exactly the message Richard Elsner and Bridget Farrands offer in their book, "Leadership Transitions: How Business Leaders Can Successfully Take Charge in New Roles." I've handed their nifty graphic to several people who are in the throes of a tumultuous professional transition, and they found its simplicity and clarity reassuring. They reported that they were able to continue visualizing its message over time to keep themselves grounded.

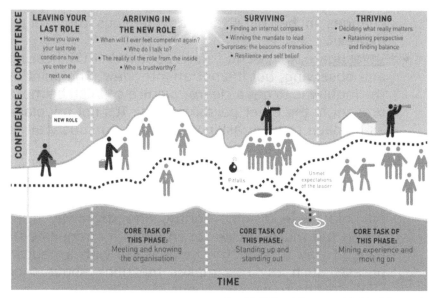

Credit: Richard Elsner and Bridget Farrands

Even with such reassurances, it's clearly a big and scary world, which is why the Breton Fisherman's Prayer is printed on so many inspirational wall-hangings: "...The sea is so great, and my boat is so small." In turbulent times, having someone to talk things through can make the journey feel less threatening.

My coaching process is pretty consistent. I'm always aiming to raise my colleague's awareness, to mobilize their energy. I give each session a simple structure that includes a few basic elements:

- Contract: I start by asking what kind of support the other person is seeking. Usually, they have a pretty good idea what would be useful, and (more importantly) what they don't want. Do you want hugs? A listening ear? Ideas? Critical feedback? Something else? It's important to get this right!
- Listen and observe: Especially at the beginning of a relationship, I'll be on the lookout for clues about what's important, and what is less so. I'll notice moments of high or low energy, strong language,

changes in behavior, and any feelings they might express.

- Investigate: I'll ask questions about what I'm hearing and observing, but it's not an interview. The point of the inquiry is to get a clearer picture so I can be more present in the other person's story. It's not my place as a coach to keep asking questions to satisfy all of my curiosities.
- Reflect: At some point the client may ask me, "What do you think?" and I'll share some of what I'm hearing or seeing. As when I'm facilitating a group, I'll hold these insights lightly, and shy away from giving too much advice (even when it's requested). A good way to start the feedback is with a neutral phrase, such as "This makes me think about..." or "I'm starting to wonder about..."
- Action: Coaching isn't intended to be an endless conversational loop. Clients come in hoping for something to change, either within themselves or in their environment, so we use the session to consider options and develop hypotheses that can be tested in the "real world." Before we break, I invite clients to come up with a little experiment they could try before our next conversation. I invite them "think small" by embracing a simple step they know they can accomplish, and then report back on what happened.
- Invite meaning: Before going our separate ways, I ask my clients to put the most recent coaching experience into context. A simple question like, "What are you taking away?" allows a space reflection and grounding before moving on to the rest of their day.

The most effective coaching relationships have a clear beginning, middle, and end. The first couple of sessions are about setting context and expectations. The middle is for digging deeper and bringing in new insights. The last few sessions are for making meaning of the experience, and bringing the process to a close. Usually I meet with clients every week or two, and we might continue our discussion for six or eight sessions, give our take. Some of my coaching colleagues stay with their clients for months or years, but I've found that in most cases my coaching work wraps up far sooner.

Like groups, coaching clients can find themselves stuck in the future, wracked with anxiety about what might or might not happen. In both cases I cited earlier in this chapter, my clients were stuck in the future. The executive was frozen with fear that others would soon discover his true identity as an imposter. The government bureaucrat was stuck in the fantasy of how her life might become more complex and uncomfortable if her writing really took off. In both cases, I helped those clients notice their patterns of mind, enabling them to gently untie the knots that were holding them in place.

Others can find themselves stuck in the past, continually replaying the slights or mistakes that have led them to this unhappy moment. Many people cannot let go even when revisiting the past serves no useful purpose...as in the Tale of the Two Monks:

Two Buddhist monks were walking together on a long journey, and came upon a river with rapid, choppy waters. They saw a woman standing on the banks, distressed because she was unable to cross by herself.

The monks offered to carry her across the waters, and she agreed. After struggling slowly through the rapids, the monks to set the woman down safely on the far bank and continued their journey. A few hours passed, and the younger monk remarked, "How rude that woman was! She never thanked us for our efforts!" The older monk replied, "We set the woman down hours ago. Why are you still carrying her?"

The elder monk, by refocusing his young peer on the here and now, was practicing a form of Gestalt coaching. The past is done, he might say; let it go. Raising awareness of the here and now unlocks energy that's stuck in the past or stuck in the future, and enables an individual to mobilize their efforts for important tasks that lie ahead.

# Chapter 17

## Closure

*"As soon as you're born you start dying."*

- Cake

Every relationship ends. You will leave your current job. A day will come when you will never again see the person you love the most. Your beloved dog or cat (or ferret) will pass on one day, or you will die first.

Sorry to be a bummer here, but because we live in a world of beginnings and middles, we also live in a world of ends. Everything that lives must die. Every experience or entity ends, and there's nothing we can do about it. We all know this intellectually, but we tend to dwell in denial.

Ends are a given; how we end things is not. When endings are handled well, people feel a sense of completeness, and can marshal their energy to move on to what's next. When endings are handled poorly (or not at all), people feel lost, confused, irritable, and stuck.

Not closing creates enormous tension, and in art this can be a powerful tool to simultaneously disorient and focus attention. The Beatles knew this when they recorded "Her Majesty," a 23-second music hall ditty at the end of their 1969 masterpiece, *Abbey Road*. As Paul McCartney sings over a lively guitar riff, the listener is pulled along until...the recording cuts off one note early. The omission of that final chord (which turns out to have been a happy accident) leaves the song ringing in your head long after the album has concluded.

In 1999, *The Sopranos* ended its long run on HBO with a tension-filled scene at a bustling restaurant. As the mob family assembles for its last supper, the music rises, a suspicious-looking man walks past the table, and then...abrupt cut to black. Around the country, people like me screamed at the television believing the cable had cut out at the worst possible moment, but the shocking conclusion was intentional. Years later, I remember every nuance from that final 4-minute scene because the producers refused to give me a comforting sense of closure. In my mind, the scene in the diner is still ongoing, and my brain continues to roll it around in pursuit of a tidy resolution.

Perhaps John, Paul, George, Ringo, and Tony (Soprano) were familiar with the Zeigarnik Effect. Lithuanian psychiatrist Bluma Zeigarnik wrote in her 1927 publication *On Finished and Unfinished Tasks* that humans tend to remember interruptions and uncompleted tasks more than completed ones. When too many Units of Work are open and unfinished, we can become stuck lingering on the unresolved past.

There is recent scientific literature to back this up. Arie W. Kruglanski and Donna Webster argued in a 1996 *Psychological Review* article that we have an innate "need for closure" and "aversion toward ambiguity." In short they argued, we like firm answers and we suffer when we don't have them. Our brains would prefer bad news (for instance, about a romantic breakup) over no news at all. Which is why, as advice columnists and Oprah can tell you, what you really need at the painful end of a relationship is closure...so you can delete that rat's photo, fire up Tinder, and move on to whoever's next.

As a Gestalt consultant, I'm interested in bringing professional relationships and processes to a satisfying conclusion so energy is available for the work ahead. I don't want people dwelling on what happened five minutes ago when it's time to move on together to whatever is next.

I see the after-effects of bad closure all the time. Sometimes it's a project that gets unceremoniously shelved after an unforeseen leadership change, leaving people feeling whiplashed. Or it can be a colleague fired suddenly and without explanation to the rest of the team.

(Yes, this can be unavoidable. Company policies and privacy laws may limit what employers tell their staff about the circumstances of a firing or separation. Nevertheless, the pain and bewilderment when employees suddenly and unexpectedly lose a colleague can be real and impactful.)

Or it can be the owner of the local hair studio who assembled his staff to announce without warning that the company was dissolving immediately, and everyone was to pack their things and leave the premises since they were all fired. Nobody had any idea that the end was coming, and the owner refused to explain why the abrupt closure was taking place. People were dumbfounded and furious. Ten years later, former employees continue to steam about the events of that day. They can't move on from their emotions because the story of their shared work life stopped in such an abrupt and unsatisfying way.

As each of these examples shows, effective closure is not merely a cessation of action or activity. Closure is a distinct and intentional process with identifiable issues to address. People need several elements to move on:

- Space and time to experience the moment, rather than feeling rushed. I often see written agendas that fly straight from "doing the work" to...well, nothing. And

# IMPACT

I've been in numerous meetings where the scheduled end time arrives and it's as if the bell rang at the end of a high school geometry class. Everyone stands up, packs their bags, and walks out of the room regardless of who's speaking or what's being done. Satisfying endings don't have to be lengthy or complicated, but they still deserve attention.

- An appreciation of the process completed, the people who were integral to the work, and the goals that were achieved (including aspirations that were only partly realized, or even left undone). At the end of meetings, I sometimes invite people to offer a brief appreciation of a colleague who helped them through the process, and those acknowledgements generate enormous energy and emotional connection. On a more practical side, it's helpful to identify anything participants learned, or name take-aways that might help the organization move forward.

- Reflection on how this experience fits into a larger context, the group's work, and/or the people who have been involved. This is a chance to sketch-out how what was just completed aligns with larger goals or initiatives. It can frequently help to indicate what will continue after you adjourn in the form of "next steps" or follow-on activities, what was completed, and what is still undone. Endings can also generate strong emotions (e.g., gratitude, relief, sadness, loss, grief, uncertainty, etc.) so closure is a time to express those feelings to build stronger connections and validate personal experiences.

Simple rituals are extremely helpful in marking an ending and serving as a physical and emotional pivot point to whatever is next. It's why college graduations hand out a diploma, celebratory dinners are marked with toasts, and formal meetings conclude with handshakes. You might also consider viewing the corpse at a funeral or tossing dirt on a casket the same way, as rituals designed to engrain the idea that a life has ended, however difficult that loss may be to accept.

Let's go back to the closing of that hair salon and imagine an alternate ending to the business. Of course, it was the owner's right to shutter his studio for whatever reason; but how much easier would it have been for his employees had he let them prepare for the moment by announcing it beforehand? He could have used the final meeting as a chance to reflect on enjoyable moments from their time together, share amusing recollections, and celebrate accomplishments. The group could remember colleagues who were meaningful to the salon's success, but who had already departed.

That final salon gathering could have been a transition point between their shared experience and whatever would be next for each individual. They could reflect on how they had grown or changed over the years, and the place this moment had in their lives. They could console one another's feelings of grief and loss, and support each other in moving on.

The meeting could have ended with a toast (or perhaps a ceremonial clicking together of their scissors?) before they walked out the door for the last time. As painful as the salon's demise was, any of these steps would have cushioned employees' psychic and emotional pain and made it easier to put the experience behind them.

As I noted in my earlier description of the Cycle of Energy, Gestalt practitioners pay attention to what generates energy, and what depletes it. We notice which behaviors might release energy, and behaviors that bottle it up. Failing to close effectively suspends energy in a kind of purgatory, with no clear way to get it back. It leaves people feeling stuck. Managing a simple but effective closure process frees that energy and makes it available for whatever might follow.

We all have our own patterns and preferences that can make it easy or difficult to close effectively. I appreciate the value of good closure, but I still struggle with it because I try to fly through the experience too quickly. My brain is wired to check-out on any process when it's about 75% complete because to me, "three-quarters done" is more than enough. When I start to feel things winding down, I lose interest in what I'm doing and begin to think about whatever's next.

This can be a real problem when I'm facilitating. At some point in the mid-afternoon of a typical full-day meeting I'm ready for the thing to be over...but it's not. I may be eager to pack up and leave (and maybe have a sandwich and a beer), but the people in the room with me still have important work to complete, and I have a role in helping them complete it.

I've learned to recognize this pattern in myself, and I strive mightily to overcome it. Once I notice my mind drifting to thoughts of sandwiches and beer, I overcompensate for my wavering interest by redoubling my energy for whatever is in front of me.

In doing so, I'm trying to pull myself and the rest of the group over the finish line through sheer force of will. In practice, this works pretty well. Caffeine definitely helps.

I'm even experiencing a desire to rush through closure in completing this book. I find myself feeling impatient about bringing this activity to a satisfying conclusion; now that it's mostly done, I'm ready to move on to the next thing.

So the takeaway for the Gestaltist is: Take your time when the end is nigh, and make space for final reflections and closure before moving on. Being deliberate in the end will pay enormous benefits for you and the people with whom you work.

# Conclusion

All that I've put down on these pages are an encapsulation of what I've learned and am learning about facilitation and Gestalt. It feels apt to be working on this just after my 62$^{nd}$ birthday, which has been an impetus for reflection on my career, and how I hope to transition at some point from professional life to a version of retirement. This book is a way to take stock for myself, while sharing some of what I've learned with others.

As I've explored throughout this book, I see Gestalt as special because of the impact it enables me to have in service of my clients. It's a powerful set of concepts that on their face seem banal and unremarkable; its potential is obscured by its simplicity.

When I started to study Gestalt, I recall wondering how I would ever incorporate all of its little pieces and parts into my already-established consulting practice. Over time, I experienced innumerable small moments of clarity when a Gestalt theory popped into my head and explained a confusing moment. I increasingly found myself reaching for Gestalt models to support my clients, and to ground my approach. And as I applied more of its ideas more rigorously, I discovered new satisfaction in helping raise others' awareness and mobilize their energy.

My Gestalt colleagues have helped immensely with that growth, and our regular Community of Practice sessions always energize me. Sometimes we dissect one another's challenging projects or revisit a bedrock concept that seems fuzzy or unclear. Not a single session has gone by without someone sharing an insight that has rocked my world or reframed my thinking...or both. I've learned so much from each of them individually and collectively.

Like Gestalt itself, my consulting practice now is more than the sum of its parts. When I present myself to my clients (online or IRL), they see me as I am on that given day. They don't see the data and hypotheses floating in my head, or the questions I am holding. They don't see me scanning the environment, looking for clues about what holds energy and what is irrelevant, what is figure and what is ground. They don't see what I'm holding in that moment from the past or the imagined future, and how I'm striving to keep my attention in the "here and now."

While I may be experiencing some mental and emotional churn during many of those interactions, I also find myself at a deeper peace. I am confident I can be of service not just because I see myself as a capable person, but because I'm standing on the accumulated wisdom and experience of countless others. I'm grateful to be in this place.

My exploration of Gestalt has changed me, and now I hope to change Gestalt – not by adding to its breadth and depth, but by serving as a missionary to share these concepts more widely. I hope my cheeky observations and silly metaphors will make Gestalt more accessible and interesting to others, which in turn will lure more people into the fancy Gestalt tent.

I've seen how Gestalt builds on my facilitation skills, and creates a synergy that enables the practitioner and the client to go further than we could have gone individually. But learning Gestalt concepts is one thing; applying them

# IMPACT

is another. It takes time and commitment to integrate the concepts into a coherent whole.

For me, the integration of facilitation and Gestalt continues to be a work in progress. I'm grateful for the impact I can have today, and hopeful that I will continue to grow and expand my impact in the future.

# Resources

The iGold Center • *www.gestaltod.org* • Home of the iGold program for improving organization performance by leading, facilitating, and managing complex change. The peerless faculty conducts an amazing five-week intensive training program set in locations across Africa, Asia, and Europe, plus shorter courses that are kind of amazing too.

Gestalt International Study Center • *www.gisc.org* • Home of the Cape Cod Model of Gestalt-based consulting, GISC offers widely-recognized training programs in coaching, leadership development, psychotherapy, and more.

Gestalt Institute of Cleveland • *www.gestaltcleveland.org* • Established by some of the earliest Gestalt leaders, GIC offers a range of courses in coaching, personal development, and leadership.

Gestalt Africa • *www.gestaltafrica.com* • Some of my favorite Gestalt practitioners and trainers have teamed to create experiential and learning programs online and across Africa.

International Association of Facilitators • *www.iaf-world.org* • The largest and most influential professional facilitator association, IAF hosts conferences around the world, provides an online resource library, and offers professional certification.

Mid-Atlantic Facilitators Network • *www.mafn.org* • Based in Washington, DC, MAFN offers a range of low-cost workshops (most of which are available online), and networking opportunities.

International Coach Federation • *www.coachfederation.org* • Online resources and professional certification.

# IMPACT

# About the Author

Throughout his career Paul Cooper has helped leaders communicate, collaborate, and connect. His facilitation, coaching, and organizational development were recognized as among the most impactful in the world in 2020 and 2021 as the back-to-back recipient of the Platinum Facilitation Impact Award. Paul is a *Certified*™ Professional Facilitator, the International Association of Facilitators' ongoing acknowledgement of expertise. Clients rave that his sessions are creative, insightful, and fun.

Paul Cooper began his career as a public affairs consultant and served on the campaign staff of two very unsuccessful presidential candidates. His previous book, *Change Agent Nation: Create Change in Your Neighborhood...or Across the World* was published in 2019. A native of Staten Island, NY, he holds a degree from Franklin and Marshall College in Pennsylvania and has forgotten all of the sign language he learned at Gallaudet University.

52318493R00108